FIRST PAST THE POST

Non-Verbal Reasoning:

2D

Multiple Choice

Book 2

How to use this book to make the most of 11 plus exam preparation

It is important to remember that for 11 plus exams there is no national syllabus, no pass mark and no retake option. It is therefore vital that your child is fully primed to perform to the best of their ability so that they give themselves the best possible chance on the day.

Non-Verbal Reasoning: 2D

This topic-based workbook is representative of the question styles included in the standard non-verbal reasoning section of contemporary multi-discipline 11 plus tests, which typically have two papers containing around a dozen questions each.

The suggested time for each test is based on data obtained from classroom-testing sessions held at our centre.

Never has it been more useful to learn from mistakes!

Students can improve by as much as 15%, not only by focused practice, but also by targeting any weak areas.

How to manage your child's practice

To get the most up-to-date information, visit our website, www.elevenplusexams.co.uk, the UK's largest online resource for 11 plus, with over 65,000 webpages and a forum administered by a select group of experienced moderators.

About the authors

The Eleven Plus Exams' **First Past The Post®** series has been created by a team of experienced tutors and authors from leading British universities.

Published by Technical One Ltd t/a Eleven Plus Exams

With special thanks to all the children who tested our material at the ElevenPlusExams centre in Harrow.

ISBN: 978-1-912364-88-6

Copyright © ElevenPlusExams.co.uk 2018

Second edition

All rights reserved. No part of this publication may be reproduced, stored or introduced into a retrieval system or transmitted in any form or by any means, without the prior written permission of the publisher nor may be circulated in any form of binding or cover other than the one in which it was published and without a similar condition including this condition being imposed on the subsequent publisher.

About Us

At Eleven Plus Exams, we supply high-quality 11 plus tuition for your children. Our website at **www.elevenplusexams.co.uk** is the largest website in the UK that specifically prepares children for the 11 plus exams. We also provide online services to schools and our **First Past The Post®** range of books has been well-received by schools, tuition centres and parents.

Eleven Plus Exams is recognised as a trusted and authoritative source. We have been quoted in numerous national newspapers, including *The Telegraph*, *The Observer*, the *Daily Mail* and *The Sunday Telegraph*, as well as on national television (BBC1 and Channel 4), and BBC radio.

Our website offers a vast amount of information and advice on the 11 plus, including a moderated online forum, books, downloadable material and online services to enhance your child's chances of success. Set up in 2004, the website grew from an initial 20 webpages to more than 65,000 today, and has been visited by millions of parents. It is moderated by experts in the field, who provide support for parents both before and after the exams.

Don't forget to visit **www.elevenplusexams.co.uk** and see why we are the market's leading one-stop shop for all your 11 plus needs. You will find:

- ✓ Comprehensive quality content and advice written by 11 plus experts
- ✓ Eleven Plus Exams online shop supplying a wide range of practice books, e-papers, software and apps
- ✓ Lots of FREE practice papers to download
- ✓ Professional tuition service
- ✓ Short revision courses
- ✓ Year-long 11 plus courses
- ✓ Mock exams tailored to reflect those of the main examining bodies

Other Titles in the First Past The Post® Series
11+ Essentials Range of Books

978-1-912364-60-2	Verbal Reasoning: Cloze Tests Book 1 - Mixed Format
978-1-912364-61-9	Verbal Reasoning: Cloze Tests Book 2 - Mixed Format
978-1-912364-78-7	Verbal Reasoning: Cloze Tests Book 3 - Mixed Format
978-1-912364-79-4	Verbal Reasoning: Cloze Tests Book 4 - Mixed Format
978-1-912364-62-6	Verbal Reasoning: Vocabulary Book 1 - Multiple Choice
978-1-912364-63-3	Verbal Reasoning: Vocabulary Book 2 - Multiple Choice
978-1-912364-64-0	Verbal Reasoning: Vocabulary Book 3 - Multiple Choice
978-1-912364-65-7	Verbal Reasoning: Vocabulary, Spelling and Grammar Book 1 - Multiple Choice
978-1-912364-66-4	Verbal Reasoning: Vocabulary, Spelling and Grammar Book 2 - Multiple Choice
978-1-912364-68-8	Verbal Reasoning: Vocabulary in Context Level 1
978-1-912364-69-5	Verbal Reasoning: Vocabulary in Context Level 2
978-1-912364-70-1	Verbal Reasoning: Vocabulary in Context Level 3
978-1-912364-71-8	Verbal Reasoning: Vocabulary in Context Level 4
978-1-912364-74-9	Verbal Reasoning: Vocabulary Puzzles Book 1
978-1-912364-75-6	Verbal Reasoning: Vocabulary Puzzles Book 2
978-1-912364-76-3	Verbal Reasoning: Practice Papers Book 1 - Multiple Choice

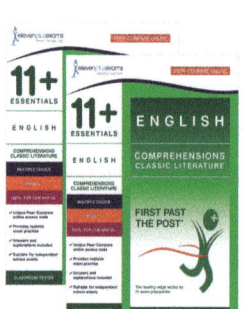

978-1-912364-02-2	English: Comprehensions Classic Literature Book 1 - Multiple Choice
978-1-912364-05-3	English: Comprehensions Contemporary Literature Book 1 - Multiple Choice
978-1-912364-08-4	English: Comprehensions Non-Fiction Book 1 - Multiple Choice
978-1-912364-14-5	English: Mini Comprehensions - Inference Book 1
978-1-912364-15-2	English: Mini Comprehensions - Inference Book 2
978-1-912364-16-9	English: Mini Comprehensions - Inference Book 3
978-1-912364-11-4	English: Mini Comprehensions - Fact-Finding Book 1
978-1-912364-12-1	English: Mini Comprehensions - Fact-Finding Book 2
978-1-912364-21-3	English: Spelling, Punctuation and Grammar Book 1
978-1-912364-00-8	English: Practice Papers Book 1 - Multiple Choice
978-1-912364-17-6	Creative Writing Examples

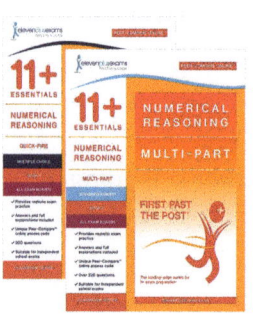

978-1-912364-30-5	Numerical Reasoning: Quick-Fire Book 1
978-1-912364-31-2	Numerical Reasoning: Quick-Fire Book 2
978-1-912364-32-9	Numerical Reasoning: Quick-Fire Book 1 - Multiple Choice
978-1-912364-33-6	Numerical Reasoning: Quick-Fire Book 2 - Multiple Choice
978-1-912364-34-3	Numerical Reasoning: Multi-Part Book 1
978-1-912364-35-0	Numerical Reasoning: Multi-Part Book 2
978-1-912364-36-7	Numerical Reasoning: Multi-Part Book 1 - Multiple Choice
978-1-912364-37-4	Numerical Reasoning: Multi-Part Book 2 - Multiple Choice

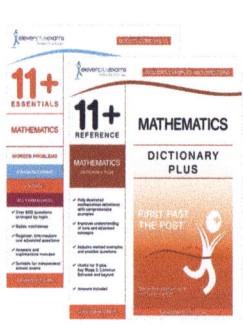

978-1-912364-43-5	Mathematics: Mental Arithmetic Book 1
978-1-912364-44-2	Mathematics: Mental Arithmetic Book 2
978-1-912364-45-9	Mathematics: Worded Problems Book 1
978-1-912364-46-6	Mathematics: Worded Problems Book 2
978-1-912364-52-7	Mathematics: Worded Problems Book 3
978-1-912364-47-3	Mathematics: Dictionary Plus
978-1-912364-50-3	Mathematics: Crossword Puzzles Book 1
978-1-912364-51-0	Mathematics: Crossword Puzzles Book 2
978-1-912364-48-0	Mathematics: Practice Papers Book 1 - Multiple Choice

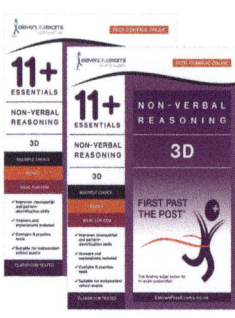

978-1-912364-87-9	Non-Verbal Reasoning: 2D Book 1 - Multiple Choice
978-1-912364-88-6	Non-Verbal Reasoning: 2D Book 2 - Multiple Choice
978-1-912364-85-5	Non-Verbal Reasoning: 3D Book 1 - Multiple Choice
978-1-912364-86-2	Non-Verbal Reasoning: 3D Book 2 - Multiple Choice
978-1-912364-83-1	Non-Verbal Reasoning: Practice Papers Book 1 - Multiple Choice

Contents

Sequences	1
Analogies	5
Codes	9
Similarities	13
Odd One Out	17
Complete the Square Grid	21
Complete the Grid	25
Reflections	29
Rotations	33
Hidden Shapes	37
Identify the Pair	41
Combine the Shapes	45
Rotation Analogies	49
Reflection Analogies	53
Cross Sections	57
Answers & Explanations	61

This workbook comprises 15 sections, each testing a different question style.

Each Section comprises ten questions.

BLANK PAGE

Sequences

In this section, you are asked to determine which of the options on the right best fits in place of the missing pattern in the series on the left. Each sequence follows a rule or set of rules regarding elements of the shapes within the series, for example: style, size, position, shading, orientation, angle, a repeating or alternating pattern, etc. Finding the correct answer involves working out the rules behind the sequence and applying it to find the missing pattern.

Example:

Which of the options best fits in place of the missing pattern in the series?

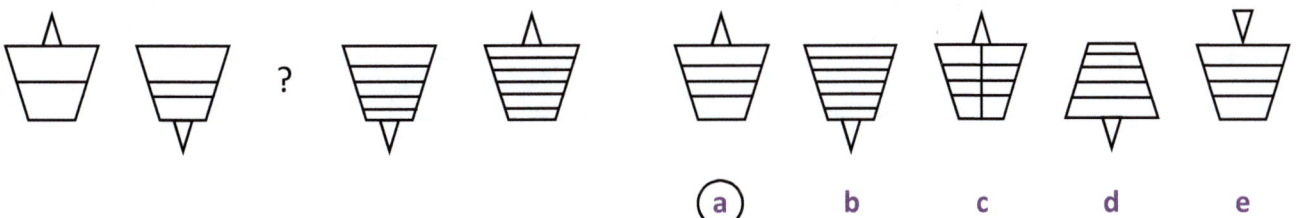

Answer: a

Explanation:

At each step, the isosceles triangle alternates from appearing on the top to the bottom of the trapezium, with its base always touching the trapezium. The number of horizontal lines within the trapezium increases by one at each step.

The missing figure must have an isosceles triangle with the base touching the top of the trapezium. It must also have three horizontal lines within the trapezium.

Therefore, the answer is a.

Sequences

Which of the options best fits in place of the missing pattern in the series?

1

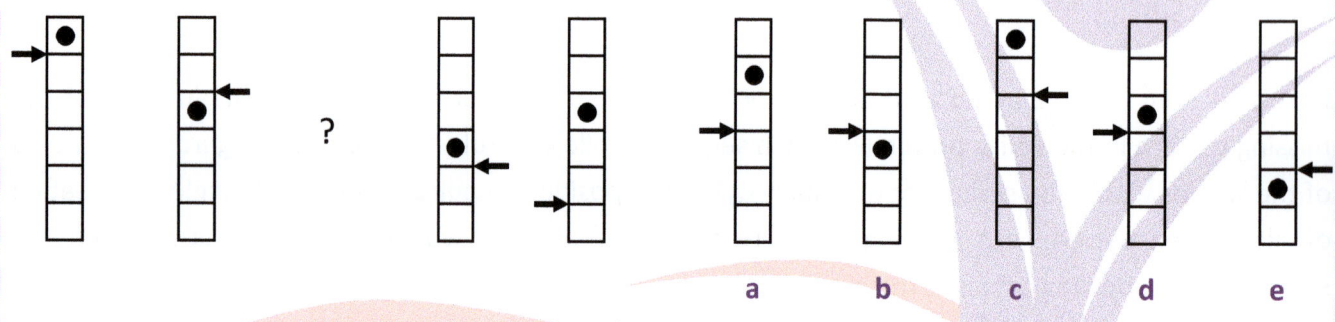

                                                        a   b   c   d   e

2

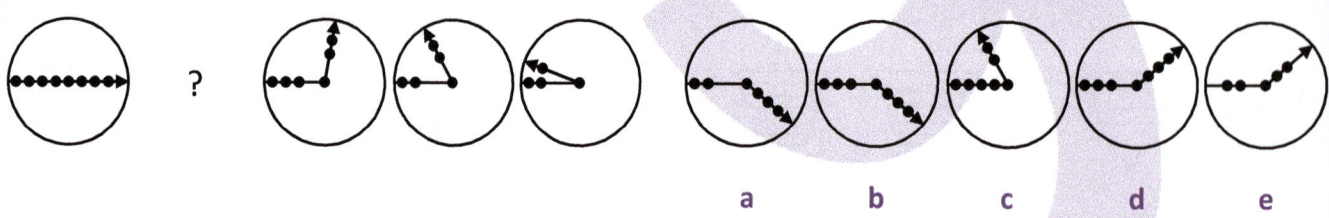

                                                        a   b   c   d   e

3

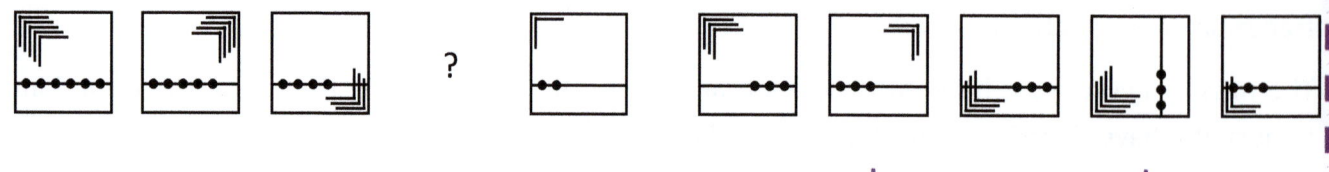

                                                        a   b   c   d   e

4

                                                        a   b   c   d   e

Sequences

Which of the options best fits in place of the missing pattern in the series?

5

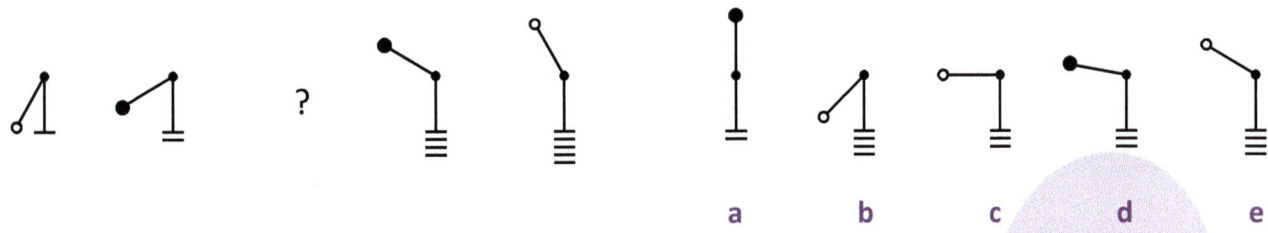

a b c d e

6

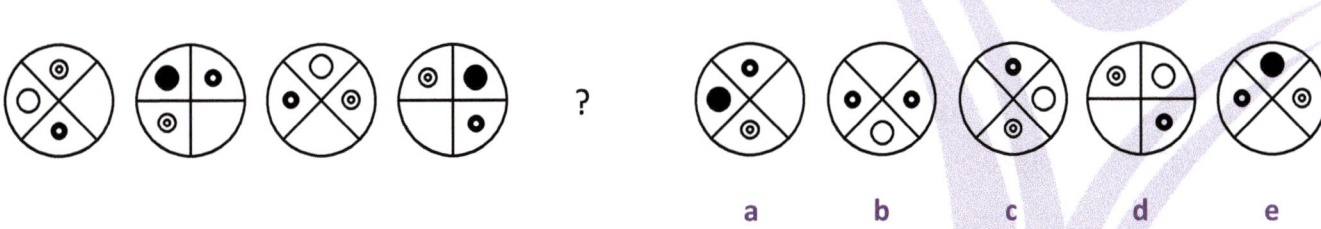

a b c d e

7

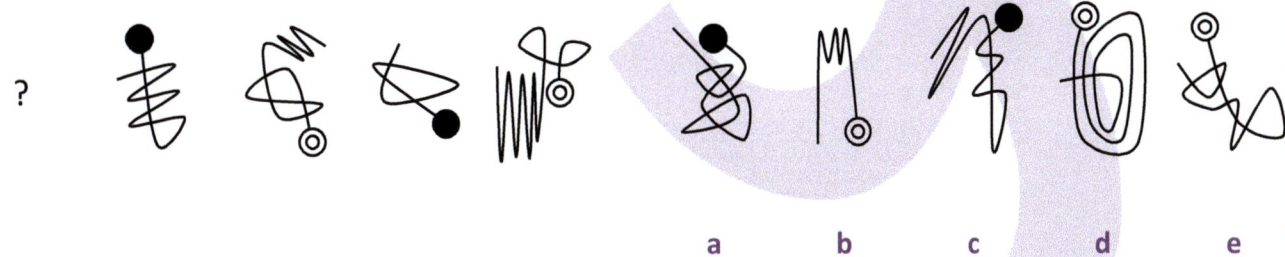

a b c d e

8

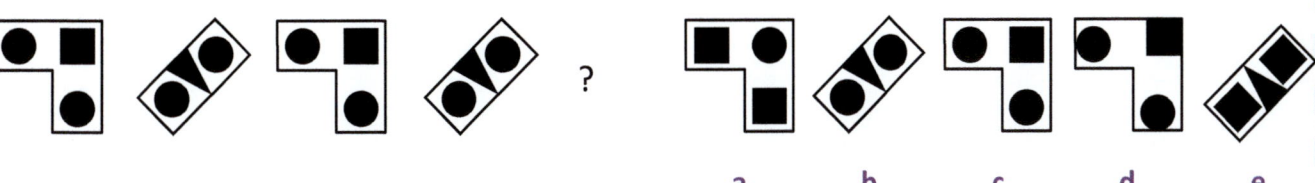

a b c d e

Sequences

Which of the options best fits in place of the missing pattern in the series?

9

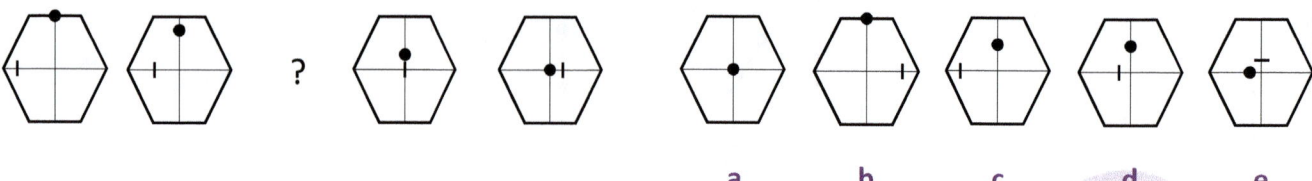

a b c d e

10

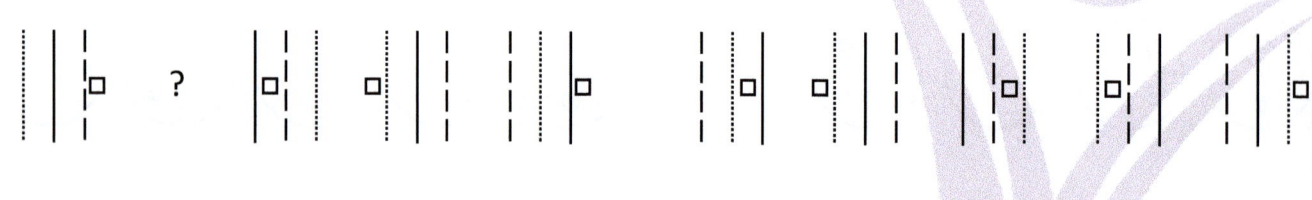

a b c d e

Analogies

In this section, you are asked to determine which shape completes the pair on the right in the same way as the pair(s) on the left. The second pair must be completed using the same rule(s) as in the first pair.

The second shape in a pair can differ from the first shape in terms of size, position, shading, orientation, angle, etc.

Example:

Which shape or pattern completes the pair on the right in the same way as the pair(s) on the left?

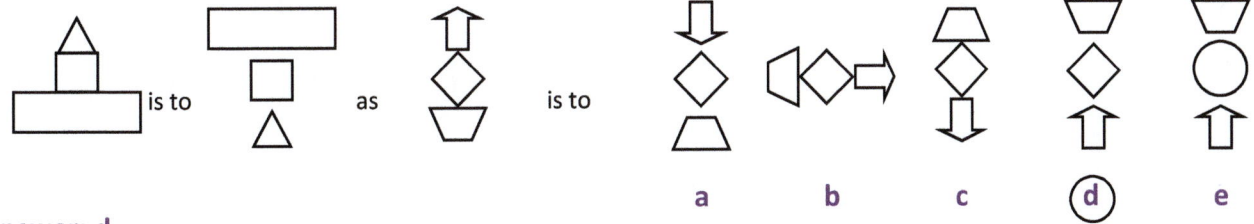

Answer: d

Explanation:

The top and bottom shapes swap positions but remain in the same orientation, and gaps are introduced so that none of the shapes touch.

The trapezium and arrow swap positions but remain in the same orientation and gaps are introduced.

Therefore, the answer is **d**.

Analogies

Which shape or pattern completes the pair on the right in the same way as the pair(s) on the left?

1

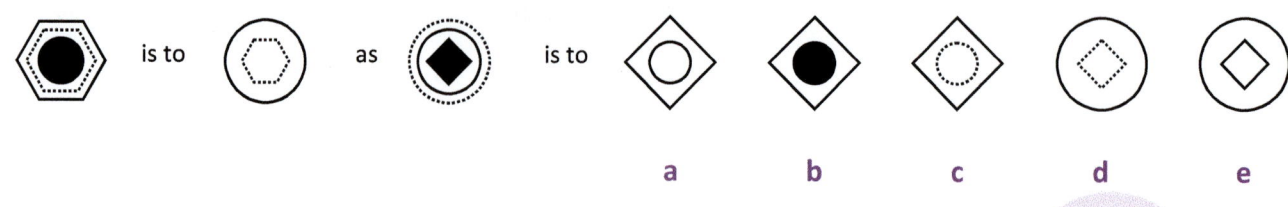

2

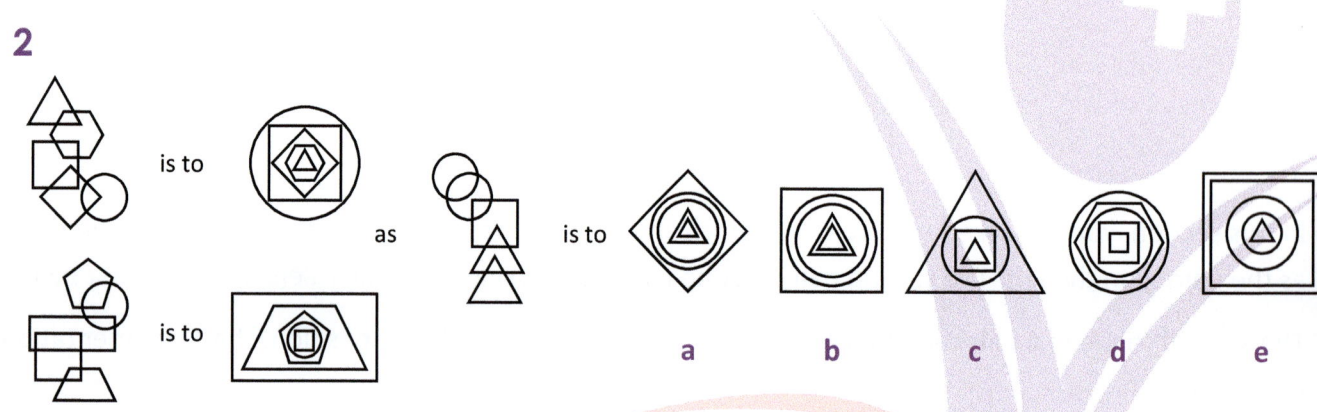

3

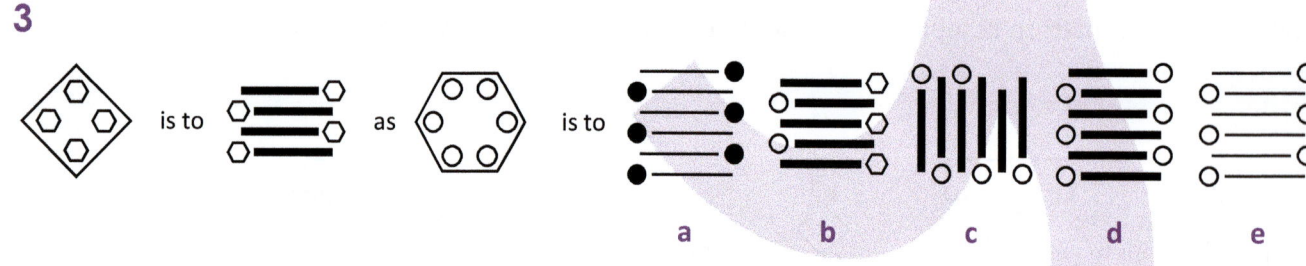

4

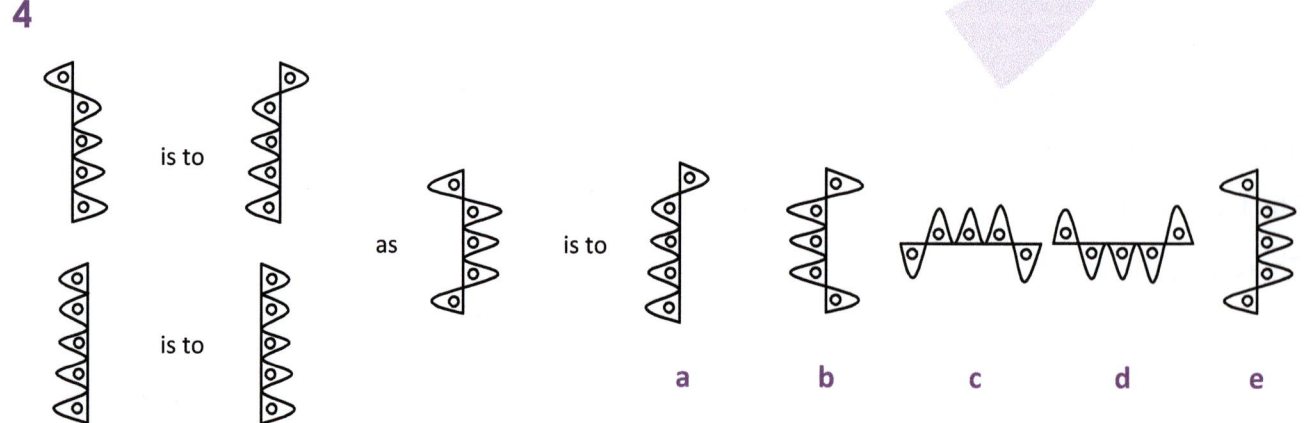

Analogies

Which shape or pattern completes the pair on the right in the same way as the pair(s) on the left?

5

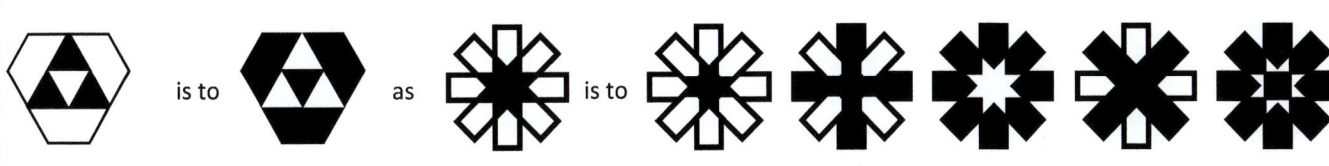

a b c d e

6

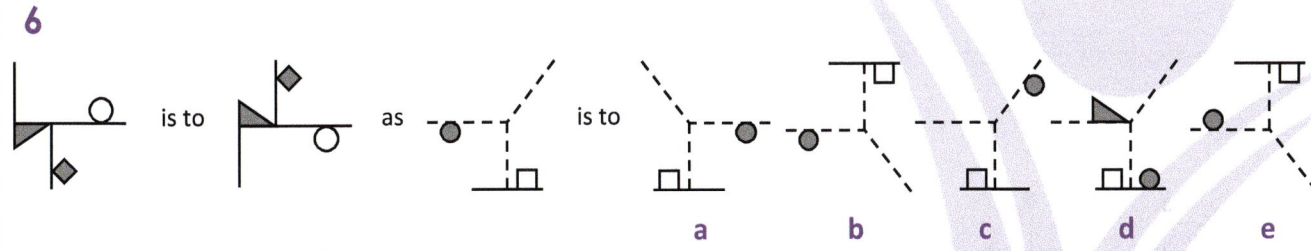

a b c d e

7

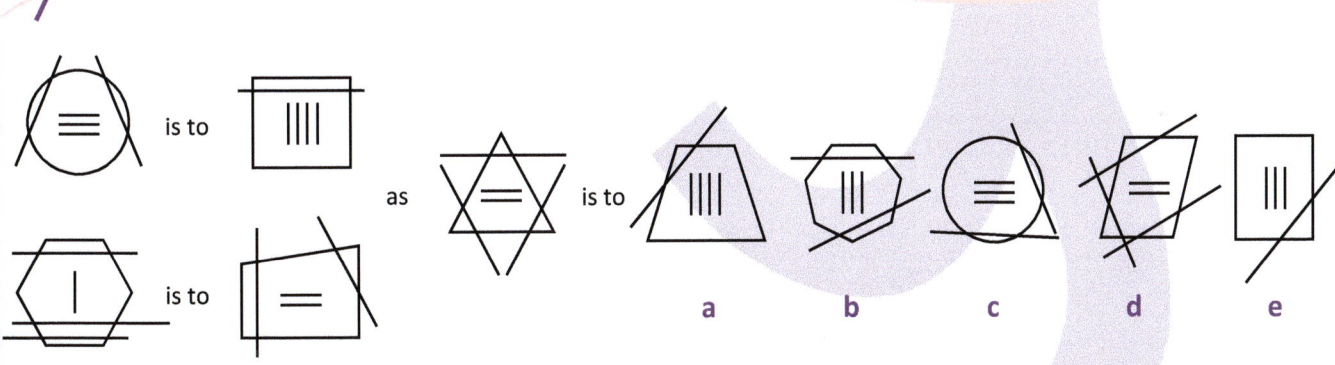

a b c d e

8

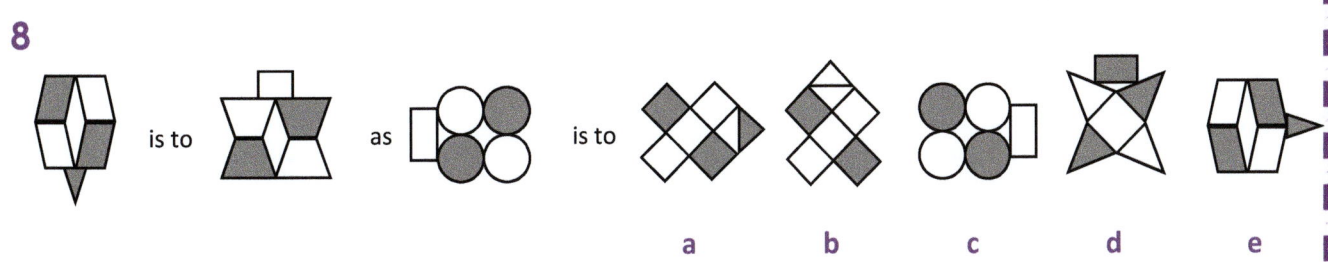

a b c d e

Analogies

Which shape or pattern completes the pair on the right in the same way as the pair(s) on the left?

9

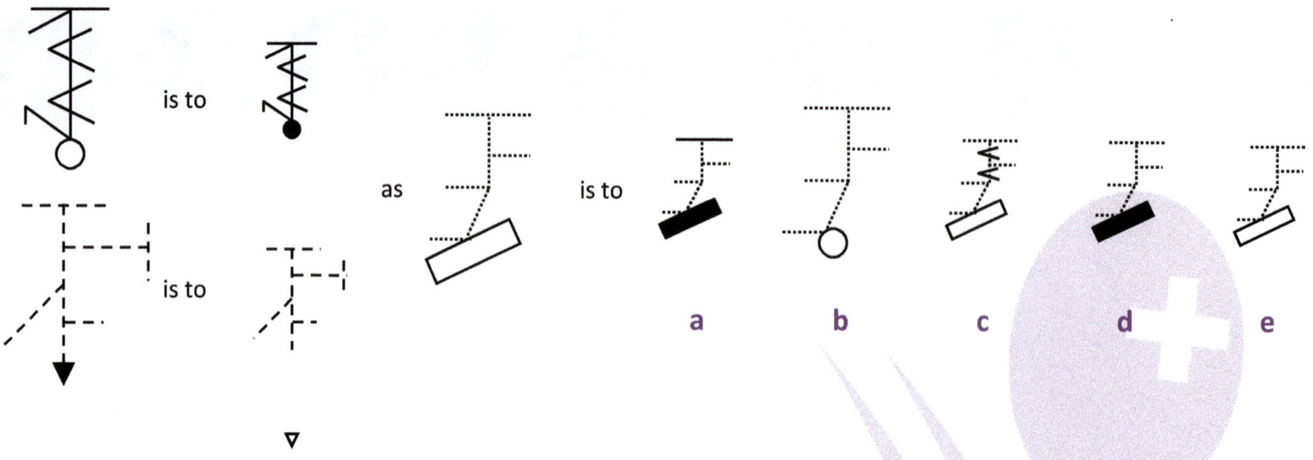

10

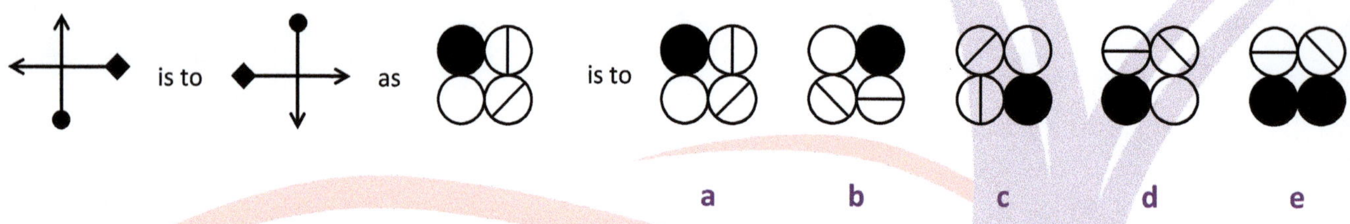

FIRST PAST THE POST

Codes

In this section, you are asked to determine which of the codes on the right corresponds to the final pattern on the left. Each letter of the code represents a particular element of the shapes in the series, for example: style, size, position, shading, orientation, angle, etc. Finding the correct answer involves working out the rule(s) behind the codes using the patterns already given.

Example:

Which code corresponds to the final pattern?

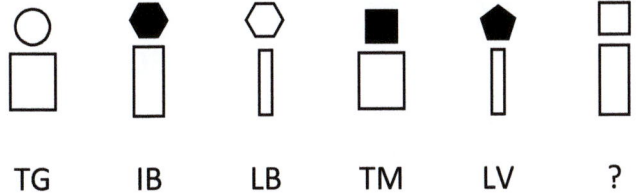

TG   IB   LB   TM   LV   ?

Answer: e

Explanation:

First letter = rectangle style: L (narrowest), I (medium width), T (widest)

Second letter = shape on top of rectangle: B (hexagon), G (circle), M (square), V (pentagon)

The shape consists of a medium width rectangle and a square on top of it, so the code is IM.

Therefore, the answer is e.

Codes

Which code corresponds to the final pattern?

1

						SY	JS	LY	LS	CK
JY	LK	CS	NK	CY	?	a	b	c	d	e

2

						QA	QH	DE	SH	VA
SV	QE	DH	SA	DV	?	a	b	c	d	e

3

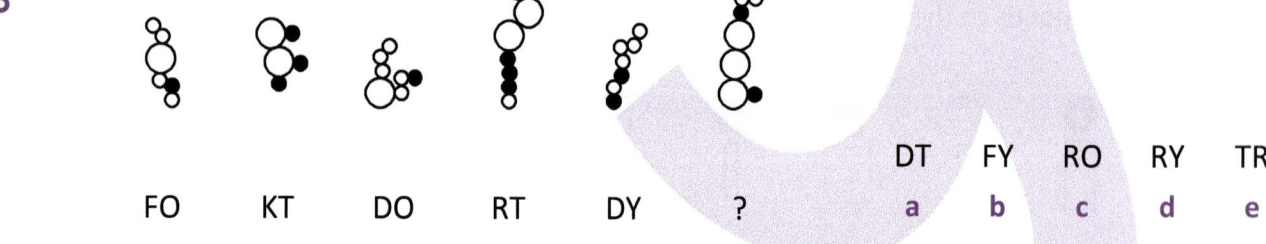

						DT	FY	RO	RY	TR
FO	KT	DO	RT	DY	?	a	b	c	d	e

4

						JS	JW	LS	PV	VW
LW	PS	JV	LF	PF	?	a	b	c	d	e

Codes

Which code corresponds to the final pattern?

5

					CK	NO	ZK	ZT	ZN
CT	NK	ZG	NT	CO	?				
					a	b	c	d	e

6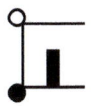

					SU	TU	OT	MR	OU
SR	MU	OR	MT	?					
					a	b	c	d	e

7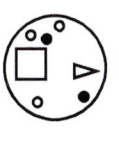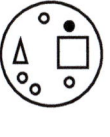

					LD	TO	LB	YO	BO
YB	TO	LO	YD	?					
					a	b	c	d	e

8

					JQ	UD	FQ	JD	CF
JF	CD	AF	CQ	?					
					a	b	c	d	e

Codes

Which code corresponds to the final pattern?

9

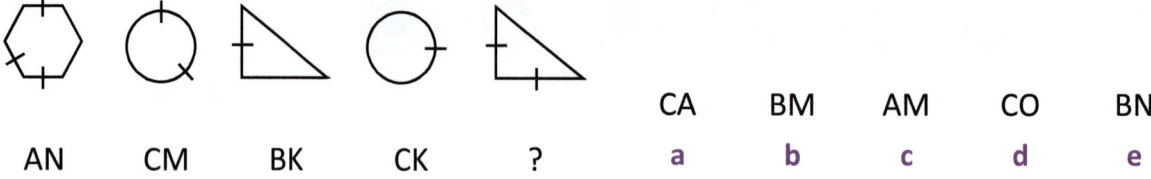

AN CM BK CK ?

CA BM AM CO BN
a   b   c   d   e

10

KZA IXA JXB KYC ?

KXC IZB JXA KYB JZC
a   b   c   d   e

Similarities

In this section, you are asked to determine which of the shapes on the right best belongs with the shapes on the left. The shape on the right that has the most in common with the shapes on the left will share elements such as style, size, position, shading, layering, orientation, angle, etc.

Example:

Which shape on the right goes best with the shapes on the left?

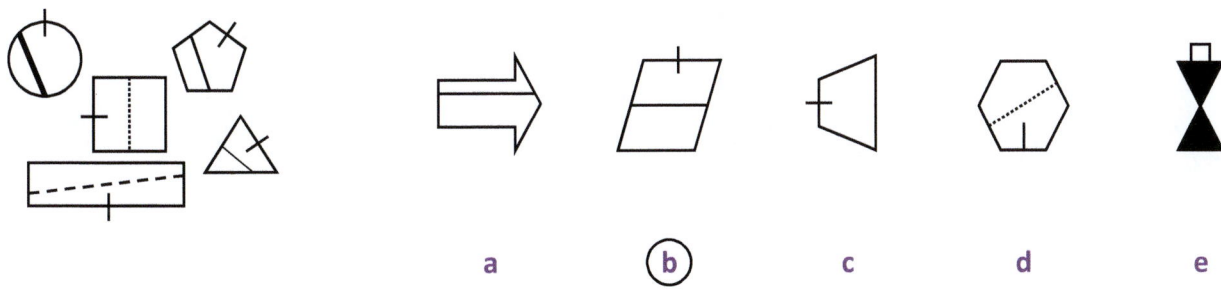

Answer: b

Explanation:

All the figures on the left have an internal straight line that touches the perimeter of the shape at each end. Each figure also has a shorter line which intersects a side of the shape.

Only option **b** has an internal line that touches the perimeter of the shape at both ends and a shorter line which intersects a side of the shape.

Similarities

Which shape on the right goes best with the shapes on the left?

1

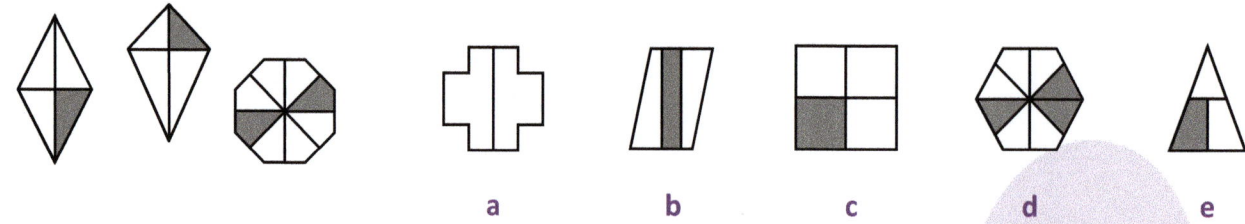

                      a   b   c   d   e

2

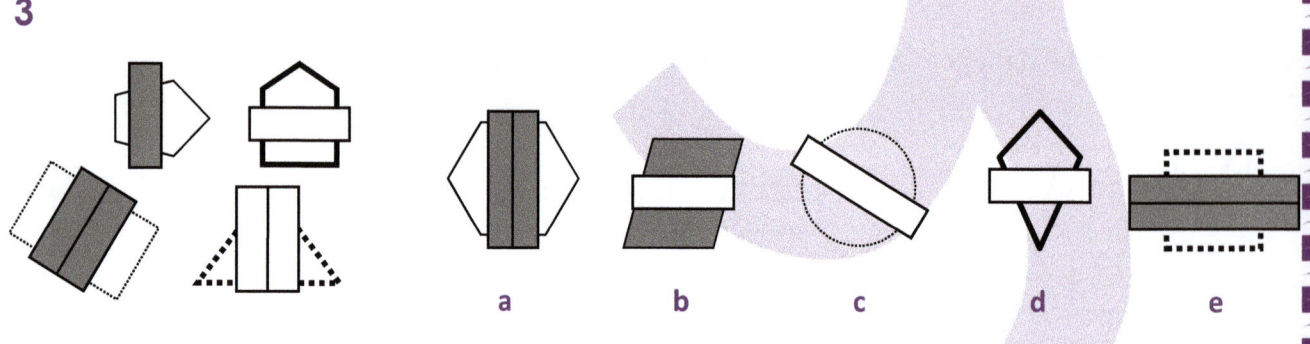

                      a   b   c   d   e

3

                      a   b   c   d   e

4

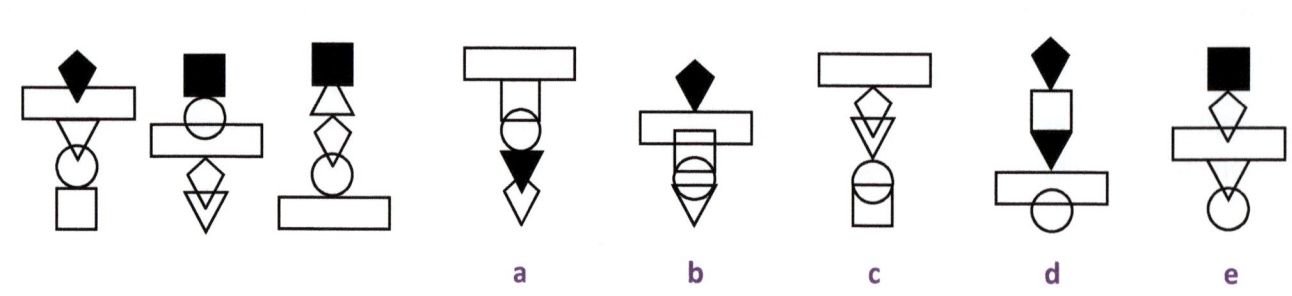

                      a   b   c   d   e

Similarities

Which shape on the right goes best with the shapes on the left?

5

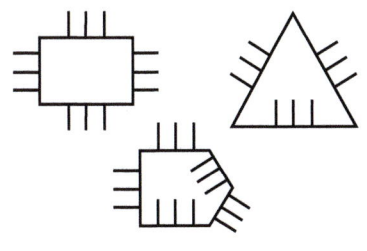 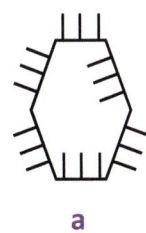 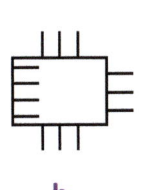 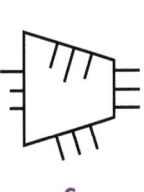 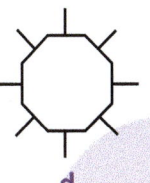 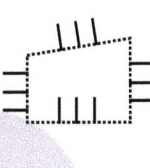

                                                a   b   c   d   e

6

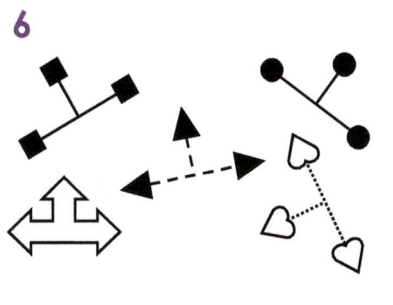  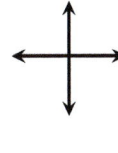 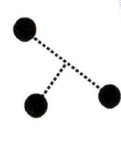  

                                                a   b   c   d   e

7

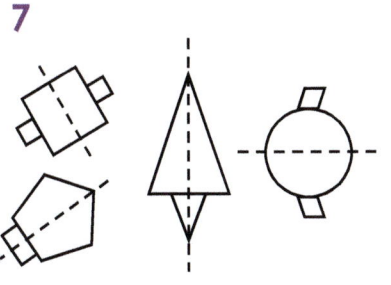 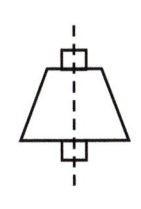  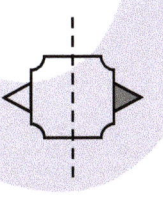 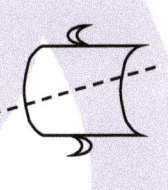 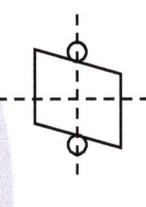

                                                a   b   c   d   e

8

 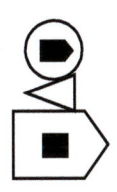 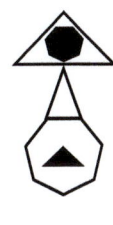  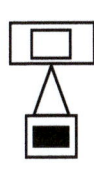 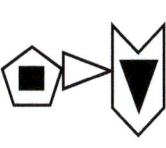

                                                a   b   c   d   e

Similarities

Which shape on the right goes best with the shapes on the left?

9
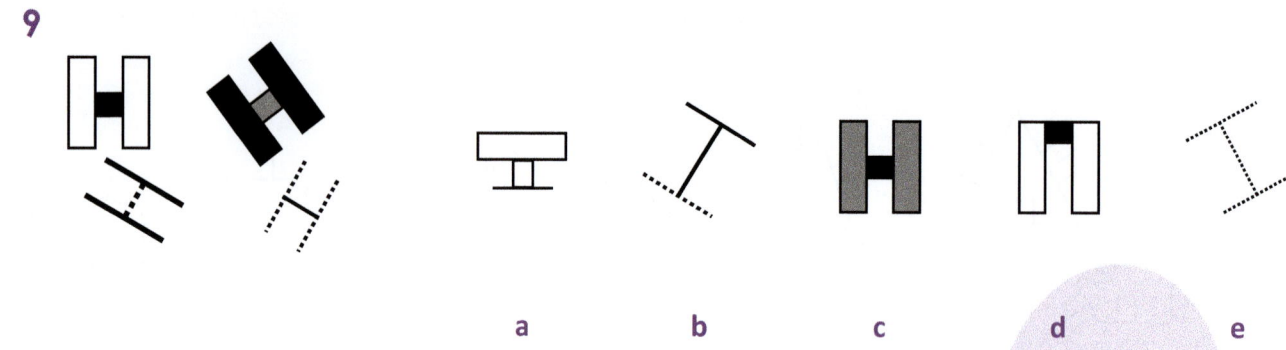
                a   b   c   d   e

10
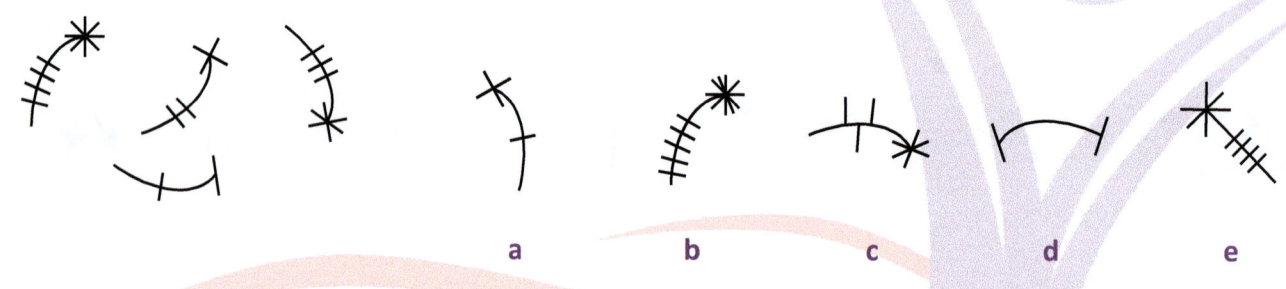
                a   b   c   d   e

Odd One Out

In this section, you are asked to find which of the five figures on each row is most unlike the others, or the odd one out.

This type of question tests your ability to determine the differences and similarities between shapes.

Reasons why a figure is the odd one out include its angle of rotation, shading style, reflection, size, position, or the number of shapes within it.

Example:

Which figure is the odd one out?

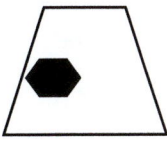 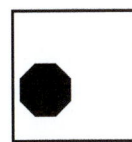 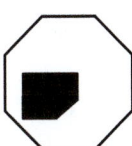 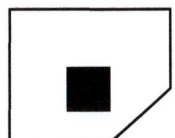 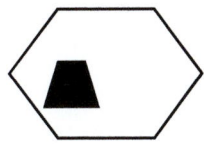

a   b   c   d   e

Answer: d

Explanation:

In each figure, a shaded shape has been placed inside a different, larger shape.

In all figures but **d**, the shaded shape has been positioned on the left side of the larger shape.

Odd One Out

Which figure is the odd one out?

Odd One Out

Which figure is the odd one out?

5

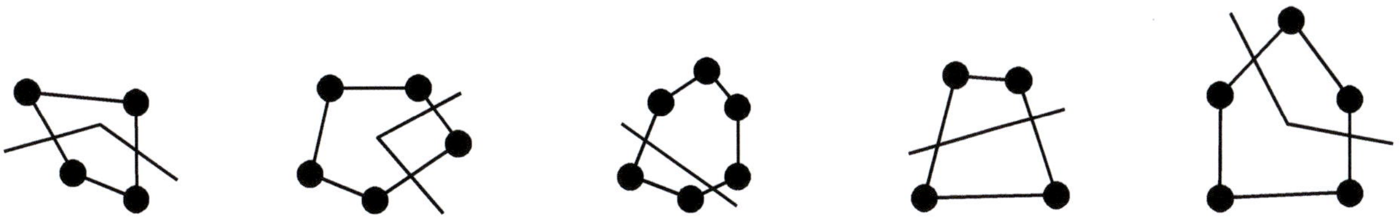

| a | b | c | d | e |

6

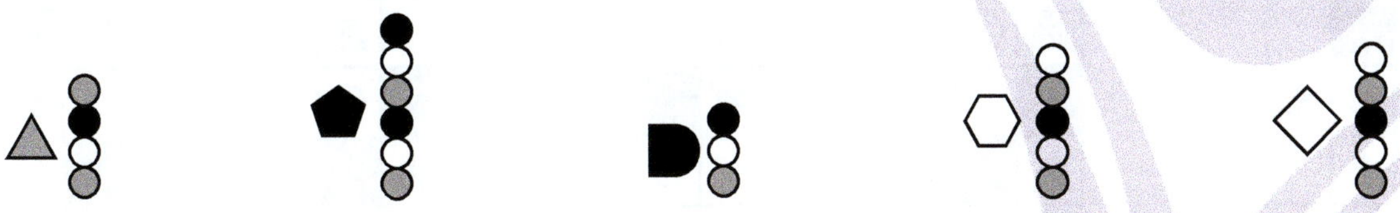

| a | b | c | d | e |

7

| a | b | c | d | e |

8

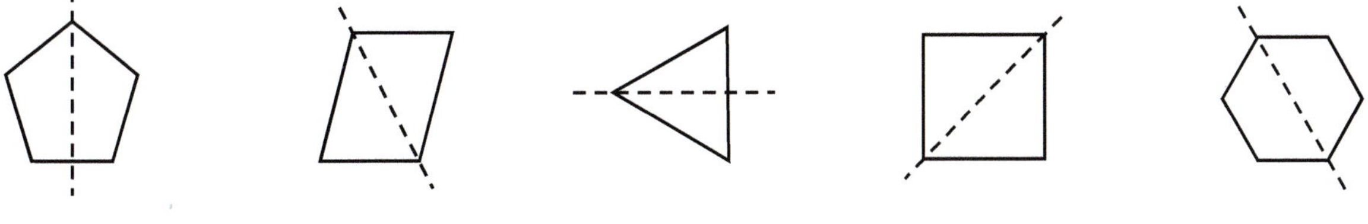

| a | b | c | d | e |

Odd One Out

Which figure is the odd one out?

9
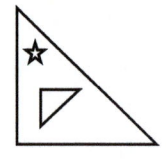 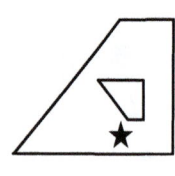   

a   b   c   d   e

10
   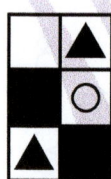 

a   b   c   d   e

FIRST PAST THE POST

Complete the Square Grid

In this section, you are asked to determine which of the options on the right best fits in place of the missing square in the grid on the left. Patterns in the grid may occur over rows or columns and will involve similarities in shape elements including style, size, position, shading, orientation, angle, etc. Sometimes the missing square will complete a reflective image in the grid or be a rotation of another square. Finding the correct answer involves working out which square best follows these rules and fits in the grid.

Example:

Which of the options best fits in place of the missing square in the grid?

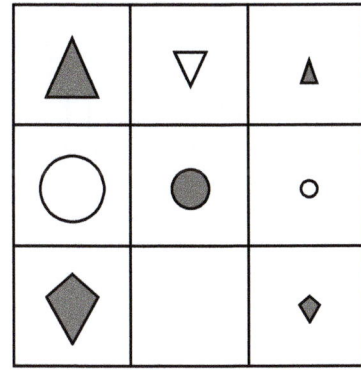    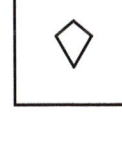 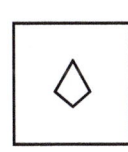 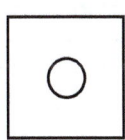 

                                                  a   **b**   **c**   **d**   **e**

Answer: c

Explanation:

Looking across each row, the shape decreases in size and alternates between shaded and unshaded. Alternate shapes in each row are inverted. The missing shape must be an unshaded, upside-down kite of intermediate size.

Therefore, the answer is **c**.

Complete the Square Grid

Which of the options best fits in place of the missing square in the grid?

1

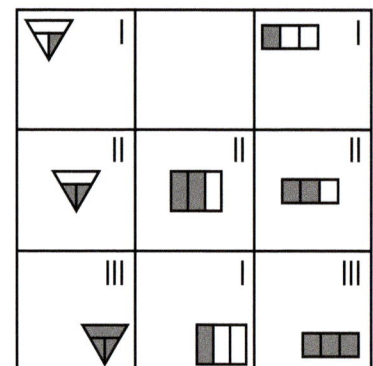

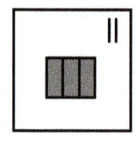 a
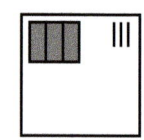 b
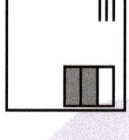 c
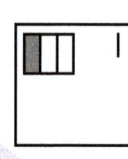 d
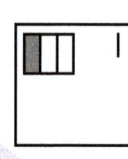 e

2

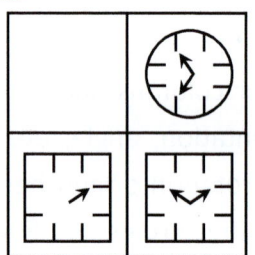

 a
 b
 c
 d
 e

3

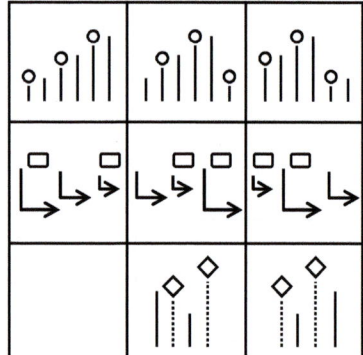

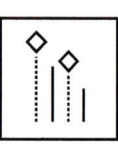 a
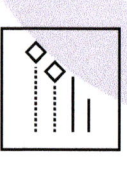 b
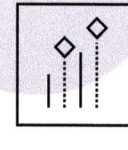 c
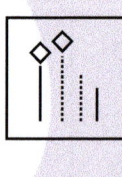 d
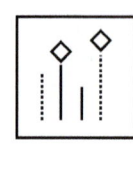 e

4

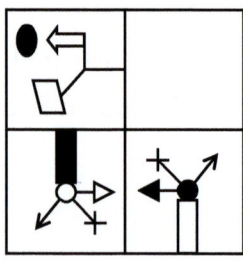

 a
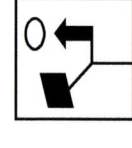 b
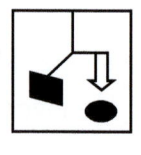 c
 d
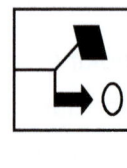 e

Complete the Square Grid

Which of the options best fits in place of the missing square in the grid?

5

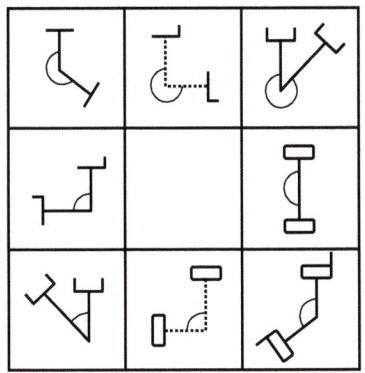

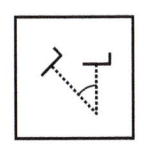  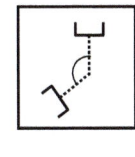 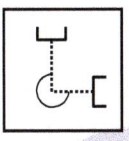 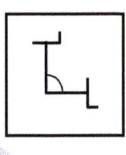

a b c d e

6

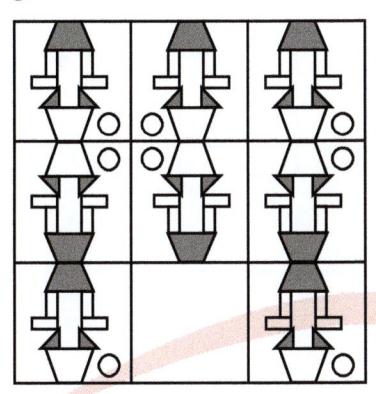

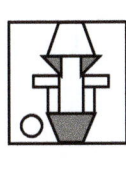 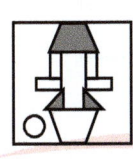 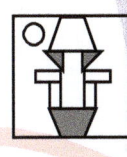 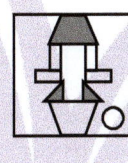 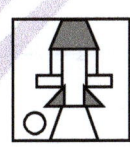

a b c d e

7

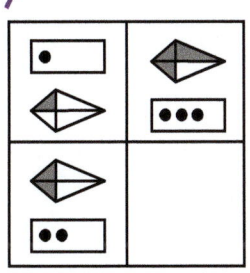

   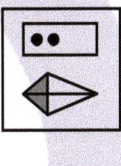 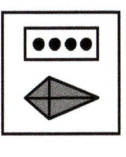

a b c d e

8

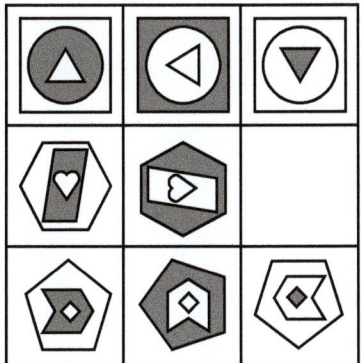

   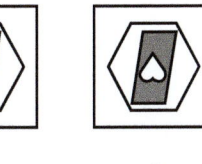 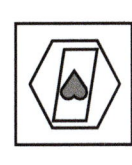

a b c d e

Complete the Square Grid

Which of the options best fits in place of the missing square in the grid?

9

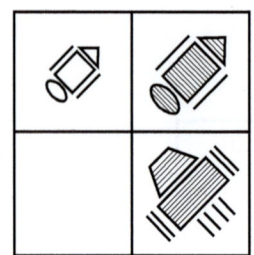

a b c d e

10

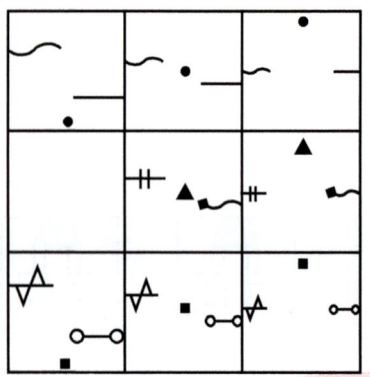

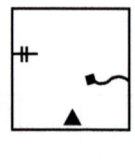 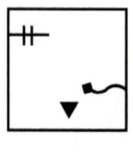 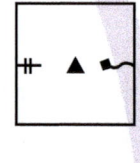 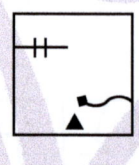 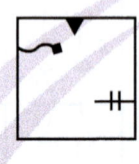

a b c d e

Complete the Grid

In this section, you are asked to determine which of the options on the right best fits in place of the missing section in the grid on the left. Patterns in the grid may occur in a clockwise or anticlockwise cycle around the grid and will involve similarities in shape elements including style, size, position, shading, orientation, angle, etc. Sometimes the missing section will complete a reflective image in the grid or be a rotation of another section. Finding the correct answer involves working out which option best follows these rules and fits in the grid.

Example:

Which of the options best fits in place of the missing section in the grid?

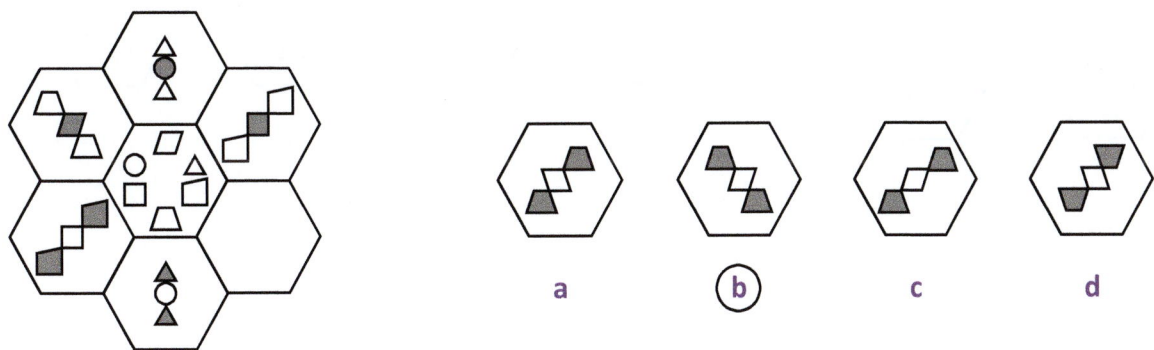

Answer: b

Explanation:

The hexagons directly opposite each other in the grid contain identical shapes apart from their shading style, which changes from shaded to unshaded and from unshaded to shaded.

Therefore, the answer is b.

Complete the Grid

Which of the options best fits in place of the missing section in the grid?

1

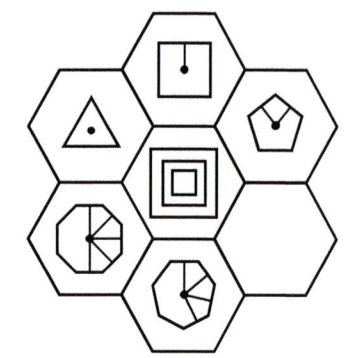

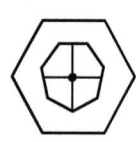  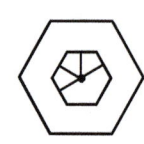 

a b c d

2

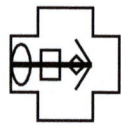 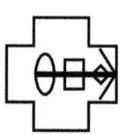  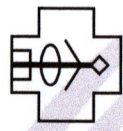

a b c d

3

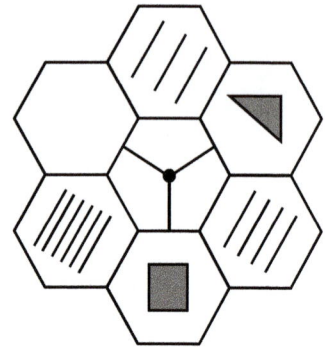

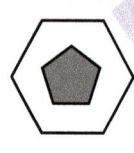   

a b c d

4

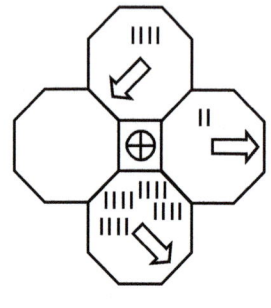

 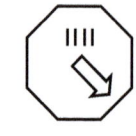 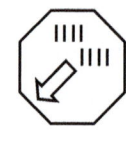 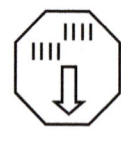

a b c d

Complete the Grid

Which of the options best fits in place of the missing section in the grid?

5

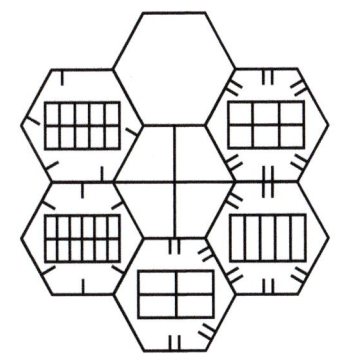

 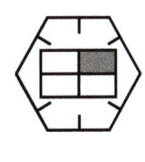 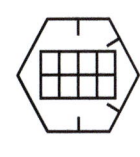 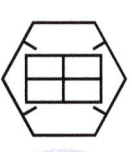
  a   b   c   d

6

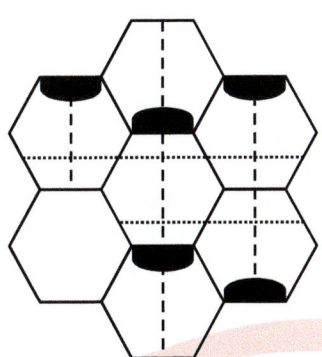

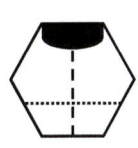 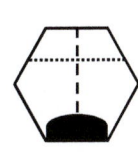 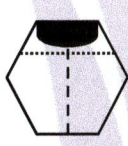 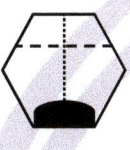
  a   b   c   d

7

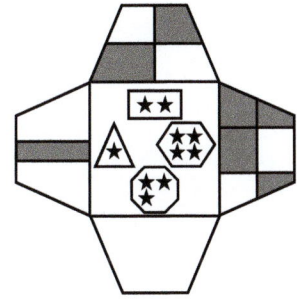

 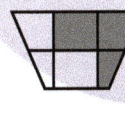 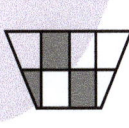 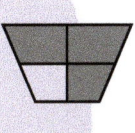
  a   b   c   d

8

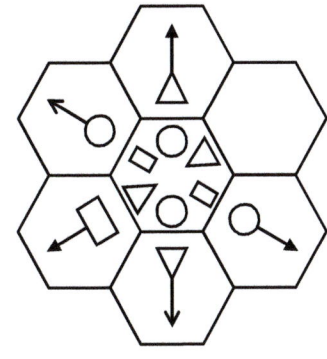

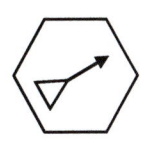 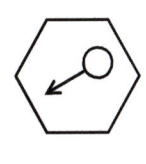 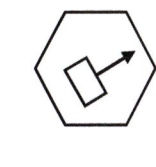 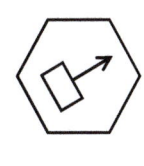
  a   b   c   d

Complete the Grid

Which of the options best fits in place of the missing section in the grid?

9

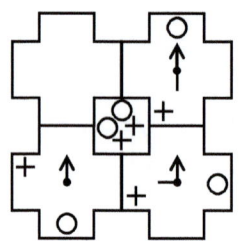

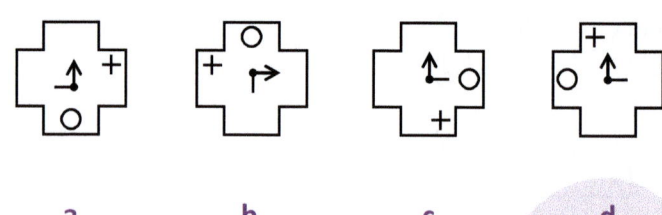

a   b   c   d

10

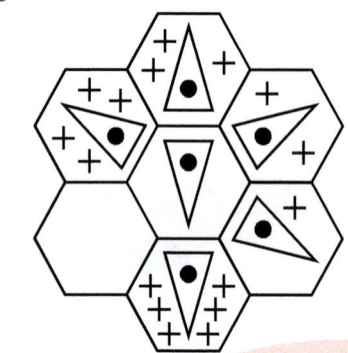

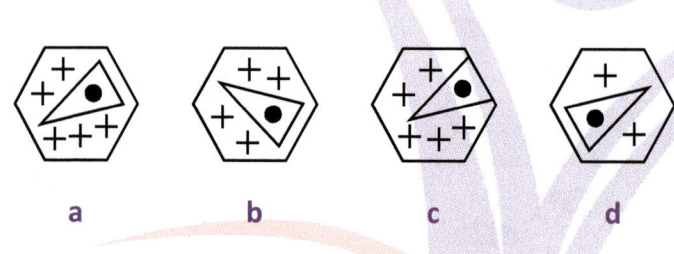

a   b   c   d

Reflections

In this section, you are asked to find which one of the four figures on the right is a mirror image, or a reflection of the figure on the left in a vertical mirror line.

Remember to concentrate on specific shape features such as a left-leaning line. The same line will appear right-leaning in the reflection. Also remember that most shapes when reflected do not give the same result as a rotation of the same shape.

Example:

Which figure on the right is the reflection of the figure on the left in a vertical mirror line?

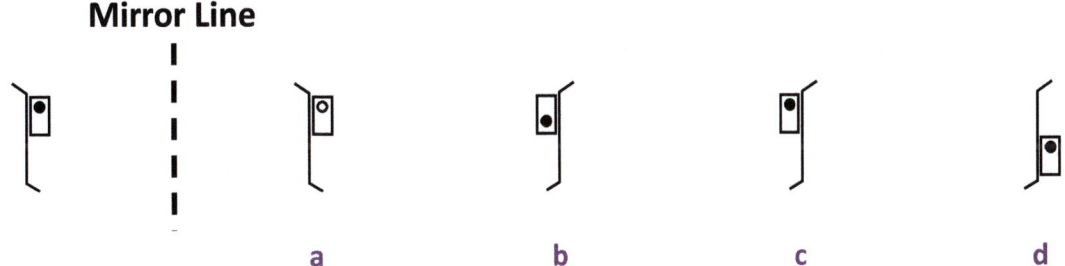

Answer: c

Explanation:

The left-leaning line will appear right-leaning in the reflection, as in answers b, c and d.

The rectangle and shaded circle will appear on the left of the vertical line in the reflection, as in answers b and c.

The shaded circle will be in the same position inside the rectangle in the reflection.

Therefore, the answer is c.

Reflections

Which figure on the right is the reflection of the figure on the left in a vertical mirror line?

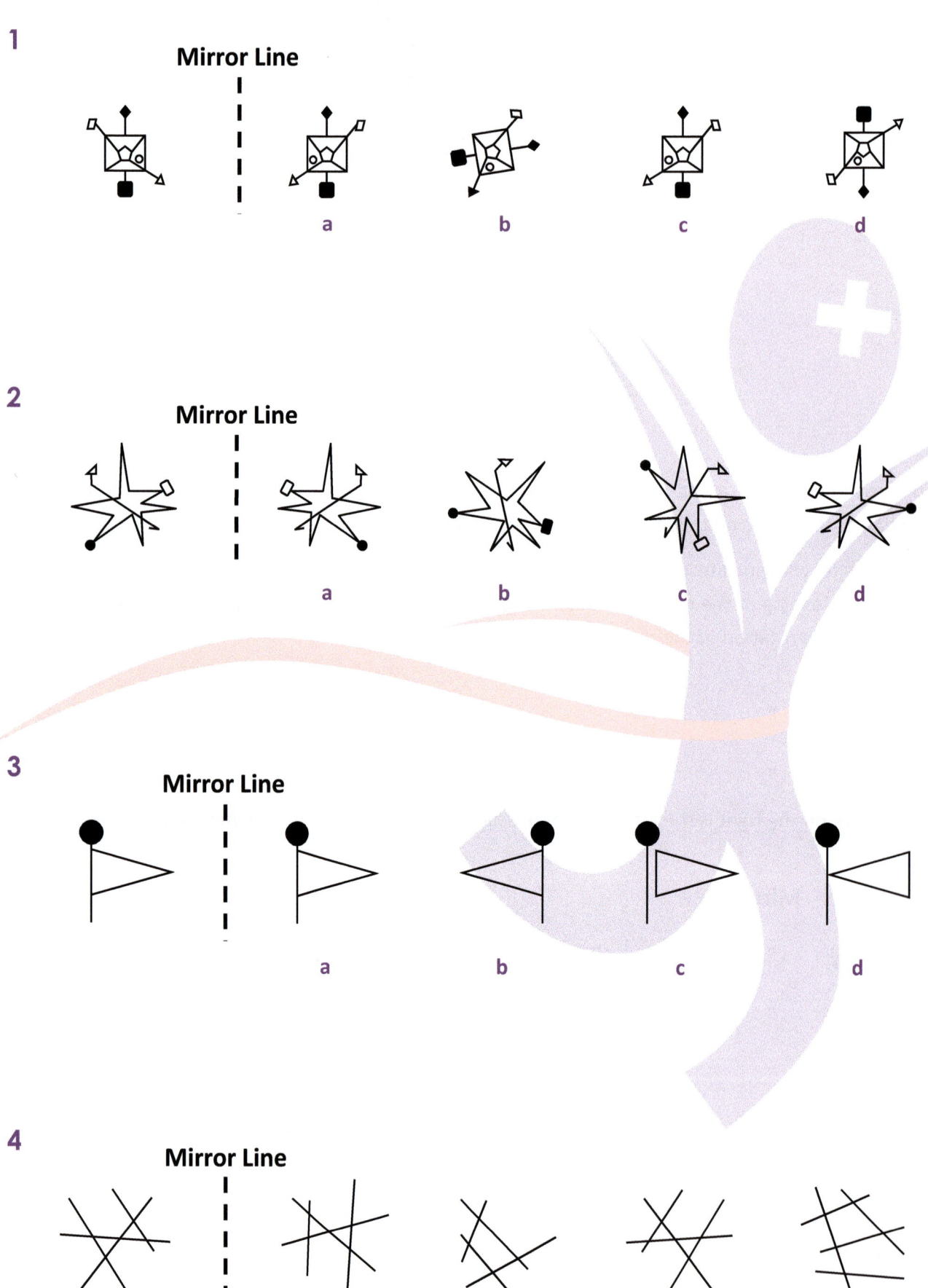

Reflections

Which figure on the right is the reflection of the figure on the left in a vertical mirror line?

5 Mirror Line

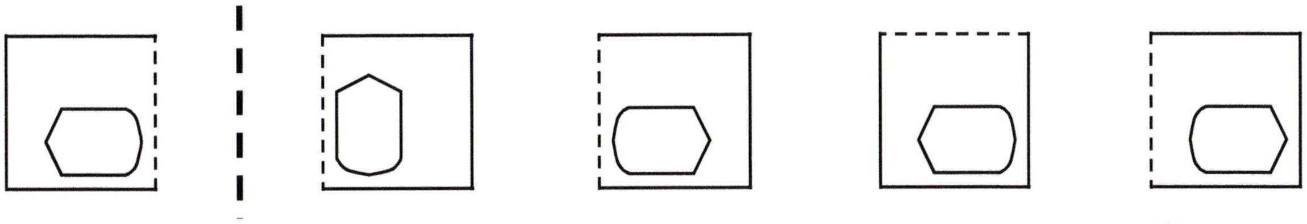

    a   b   c   d

6 Mirror Line

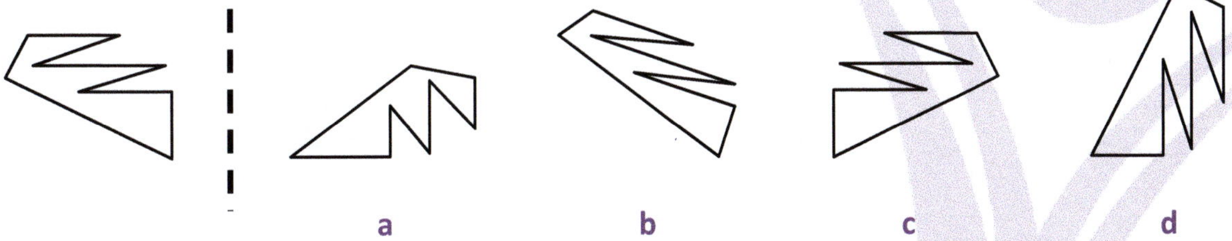

    a   b   c   d

7 Mirror Line

    a   b   c   d

8 Mirror Line

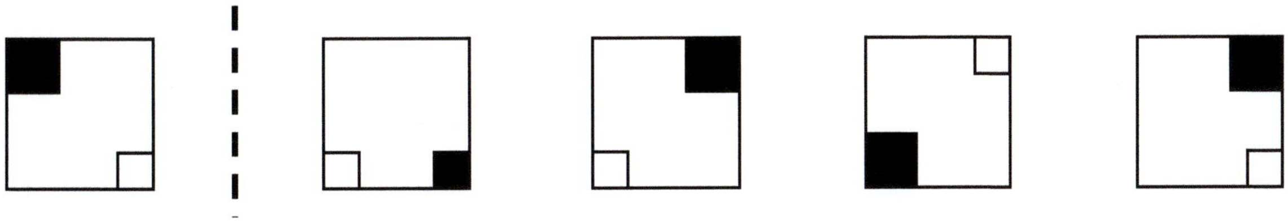

    a   b   c   d

Reflections

Which figure on the right is the reflection of the figure on the left in a vertical mirror line?

9

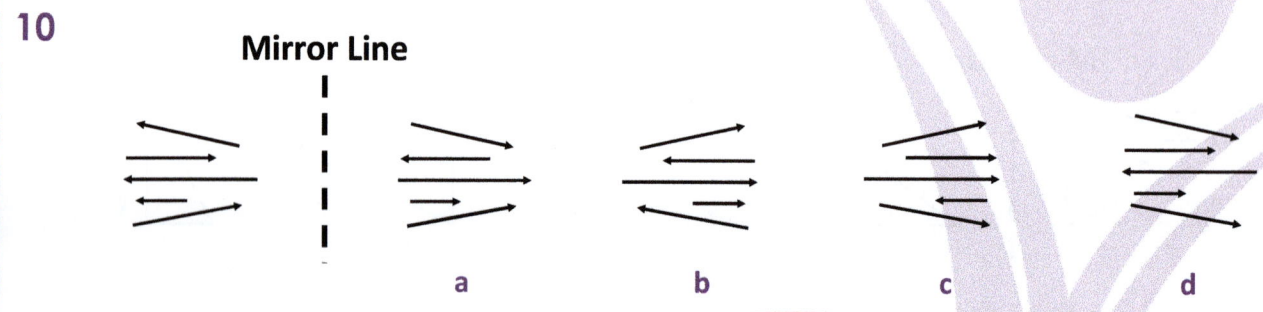

10

Rotations

In this section, you are asked to find which one of the four figures on the right is exactly the same as the figure on the left after a rotation has taken place.

Remember that most shapes, when rotated, do not give the same result as a reflection of the same shape.

Example:

Which figure on the right is a rotation of the figure on the left?

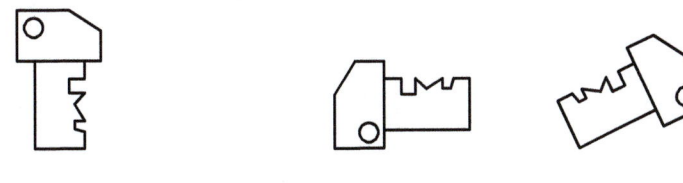 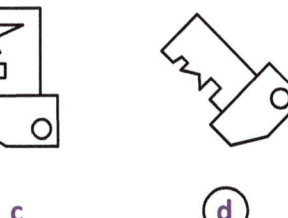

a b c d

Answer: d

Explanation:

Option a has been rotated anticlockwise by 90 degrees but the circle is shown in the wrong corner.

The rotation in option b is of the figure's mirror image.

Option c has been rotated through 180 degrees but the jagged edge has a different pattern.

Option d shows a correct 135 degree clockwise rotation with no other changes to the original figure.

Rotations

Which figure on the right is a rotation of the figure on the left?

1

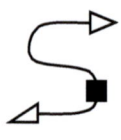 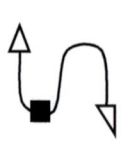  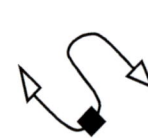 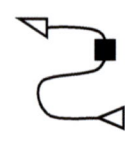

                                  a   b   c   d

2

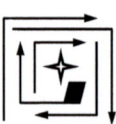    

                                  a   b   c   d

3

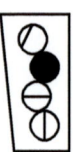  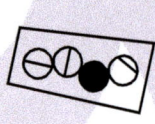 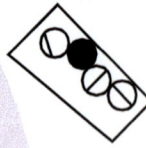

                                  a   b   c   d

4

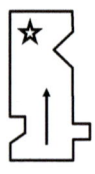  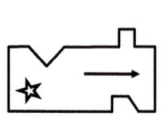 

                                  a   b   c   d

Rotations

Which figure on the right is a rotation of the figure on the left?

5

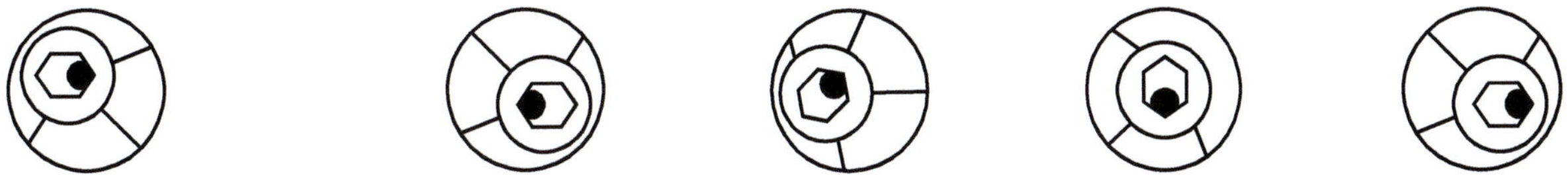

          a   b   c   d

6

          a   b   c   d

7

          a   b   c   d

8

          a   b   c   d

Rotations

Which figure on the right is a rotation of the figure on the left?

9

                      a   b   c   d

10

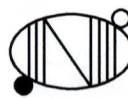 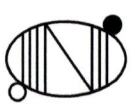  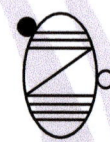 

                      a   b   c   d

Hidden Shapes

In this section, you are asked to find a particular shape hidden within one of the more complex figures on the right.

Straightforward questions test your ability to match a shape **exactly**, as in the example below.

More difficult questions involve the changing of one or more of the target shape's elements such as size, shading, orientation or angle. An exact match is always preferred, if possible.

Remember, if present, an exact match is always the best answer. Otherwise, look for the option containing the target shape with minimal modification.

Example:

In which of the figures on the right is the shape on the left hidden?

       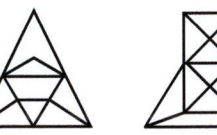   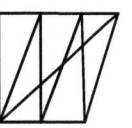   

                  a   b   c   d   e

Answer: c

Explanation:

Narrower and taller versions of the target diamond shape can be viewed in options a and b.

Option **c**, however, contains an unchanged, exact copy, shown in purple below.

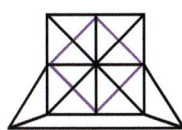

Hidden Shapes

In which of the figures on the right is the shape on the left hidden?

1

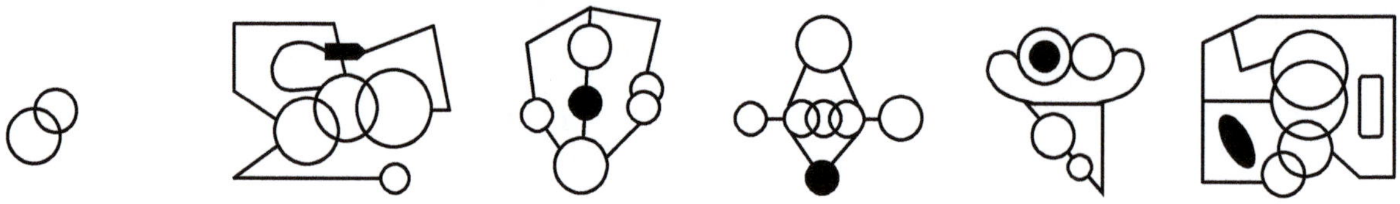

    a   b   c   d   e

2

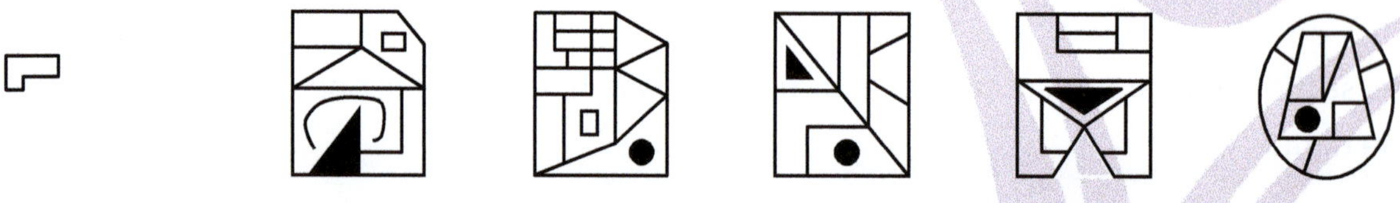

    a   b   c   d   e

3

    a   b   c   d   e

4

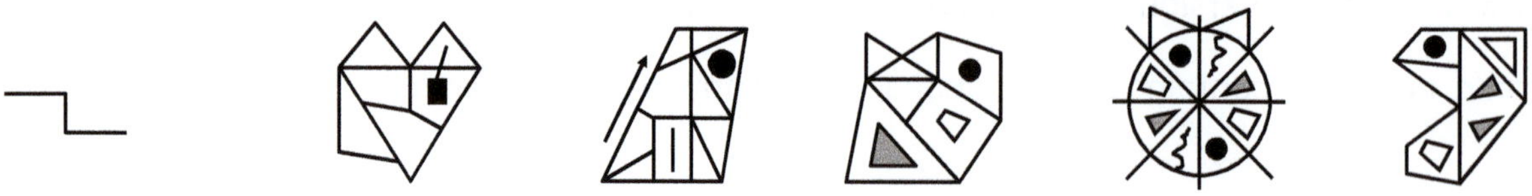

    a   b   c   d   e

Hidden Shapes

In which of the figures on the right is the shape on the left hidden?

5

                      a   b   c   d   e

6

x x o	o x o x	x x x o	o o x o	x o x o	x x x x
o o x	o o o x	o x o o	x x x o	o x o x	o o o x
	x o x x	x o o x	x o o x	x o x x	x o x o

                      a   b   c   d   e

7
 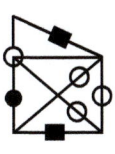 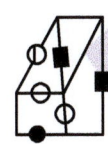   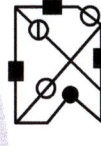

                      a   b   c   d   e

8
 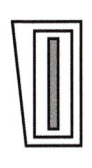    

                      a   b   c   d   e

Hidden Shapes

In which of the figures on the right is the shape on the left hidden?

9

 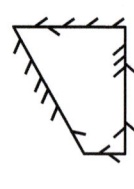 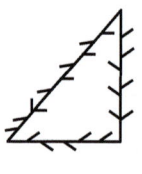  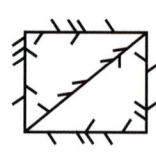 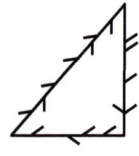

                                  a   b   c   d   e

10

                                  a   b   c   d   e

Identify the Pair

In this section, you are asked to find which two figures of the five options are the same.

Look for obvious element differences to eliminate certain options quickly.

Remember also that two figures can be at different angles but still be identical.

Example:

Which two figures are the same?

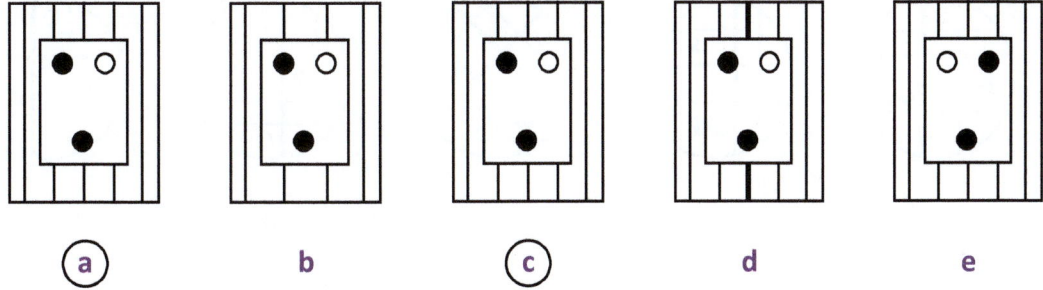

Answer: a & c

Explanation:

Options b, d and e can be eliminated due to an incorrect number of vertical lines in b, the wrong line thickness in d, and a different circle shading pattern in e.

Options a & c are an exact match and therefore the correct answer.

Identify the Pair

Which two figures are the same?

1

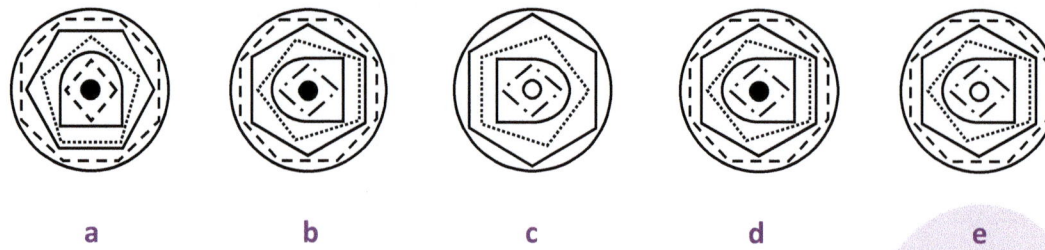

a   b   c   d   e

2

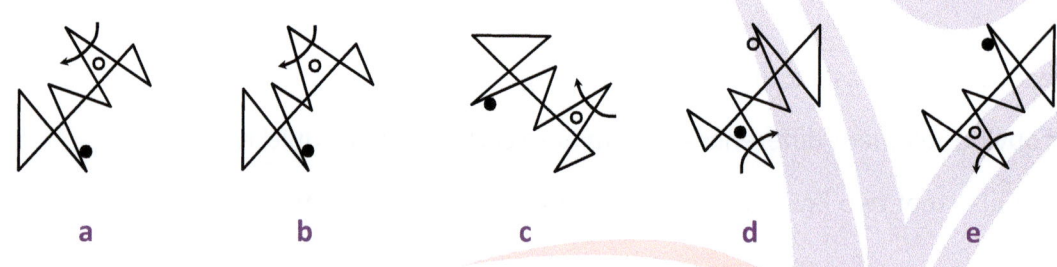

a   b   c   d   e

3

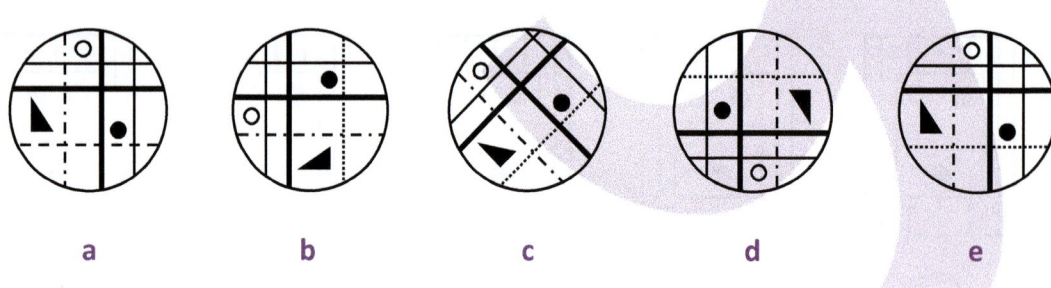

a   b   c   d   e

4

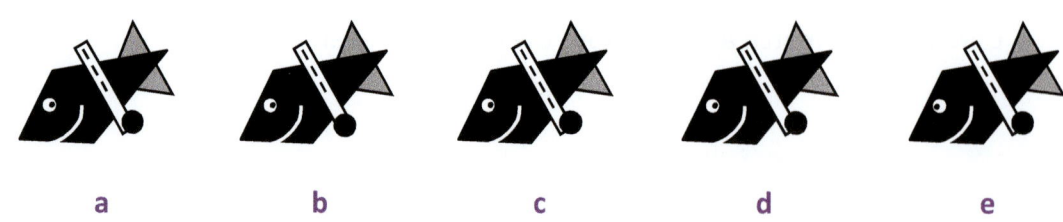

a   b   c   d   e

Identify the Pair

Which two figures are the same?

5

a b c d e

6

a b c d e

7

 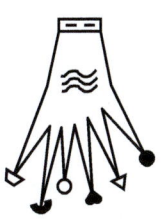  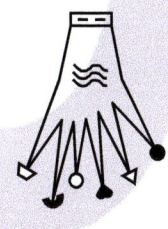 

a b c d e

8

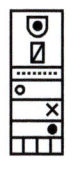 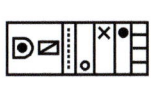 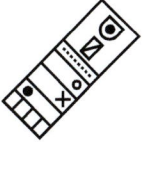 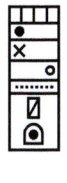 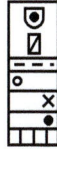

a b c d e

Identify the Pair

Which two figures are the same?

9

   a   b   c   d   e

10

   a   b   c   d   e

Combine the Shapes

In this section, you are asked to determine which of the shapes on the right is formed from the two shapes on the left.

Either shape on the left can be rotated, reflected or transparent, but neither can be altered in size or shading.

Example:

Which shape on the right has been formed from the two shapes on the left?

a　　b　　c　　d　　e

Answer: e

Explanation:

When the first shape is rotated through 90 degrees and placed inside the bottom of the second shape, answer e is produced.

Combine the Shapes

Which shape on the right has been formed from the two shapes on the left?

1

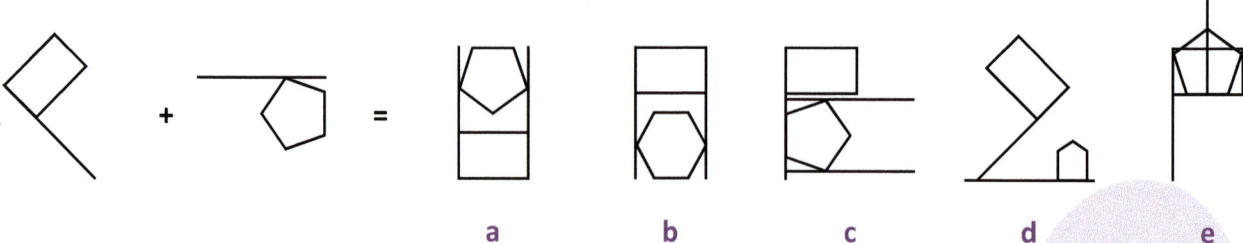

        a   b   c   d   e

2

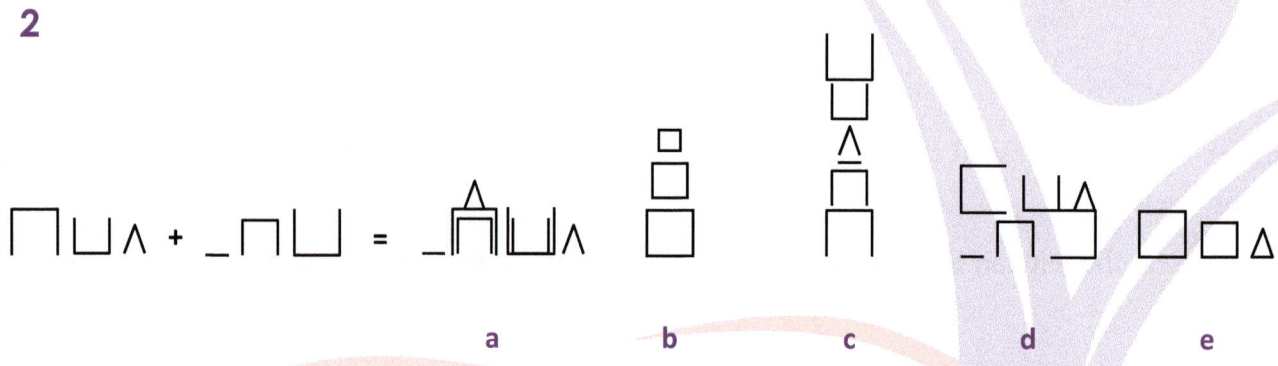

        a   b   c   d   e

3

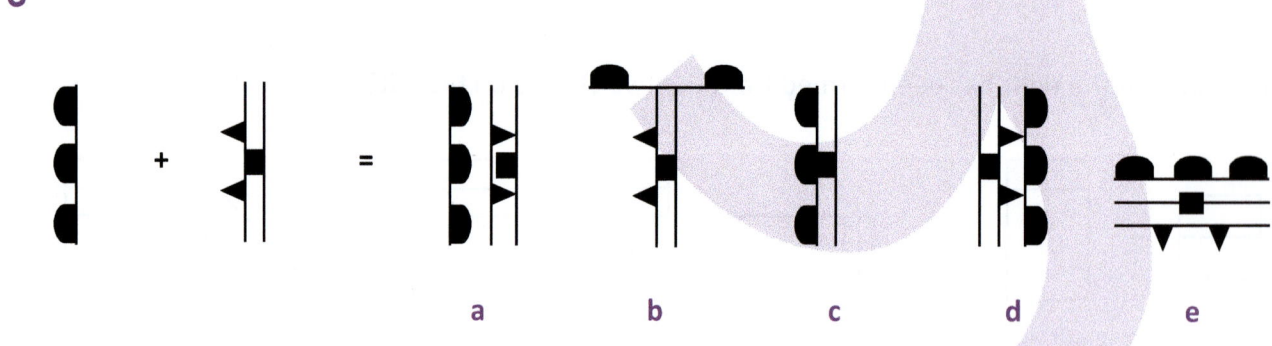

        a   b   c   d   e

4

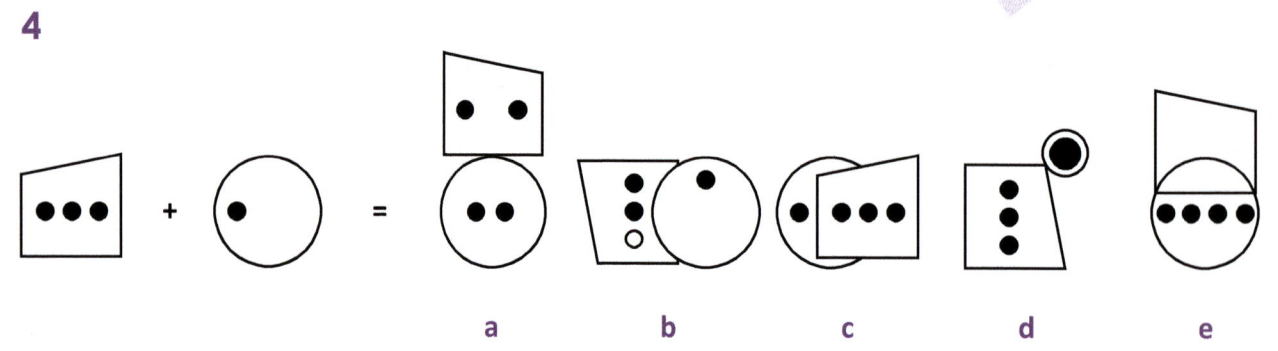

        a   b   c   d   e

Combine the Shapes

Which shape on the right has been formed from the two shapes on the left?

5

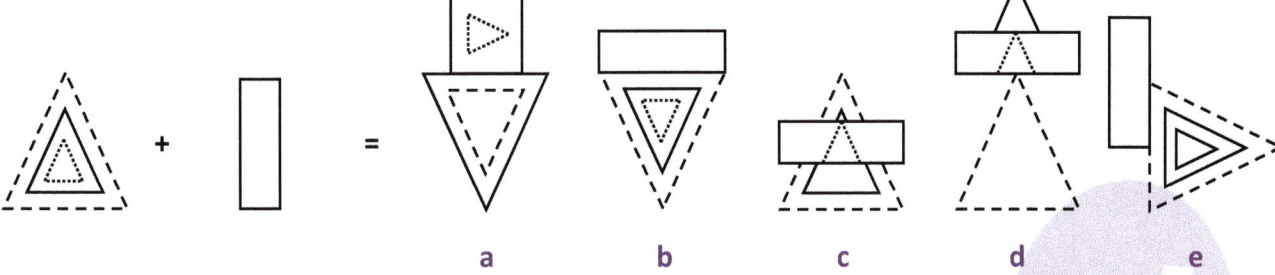

6

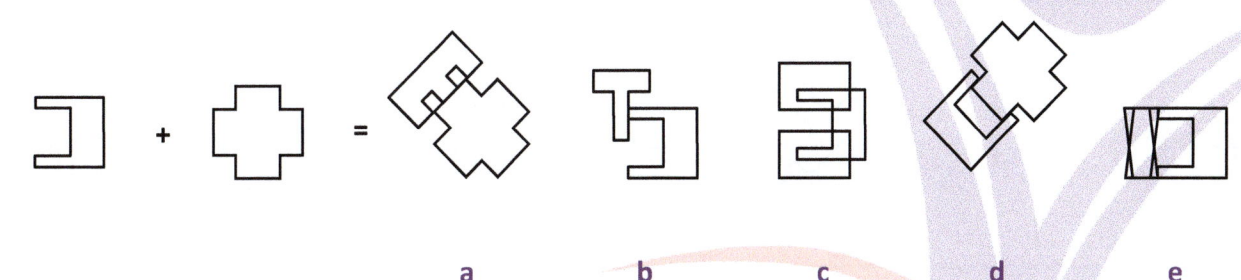

7

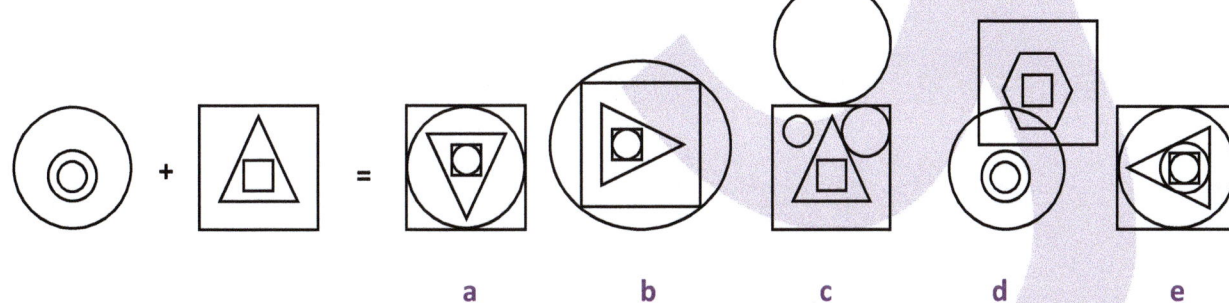

8

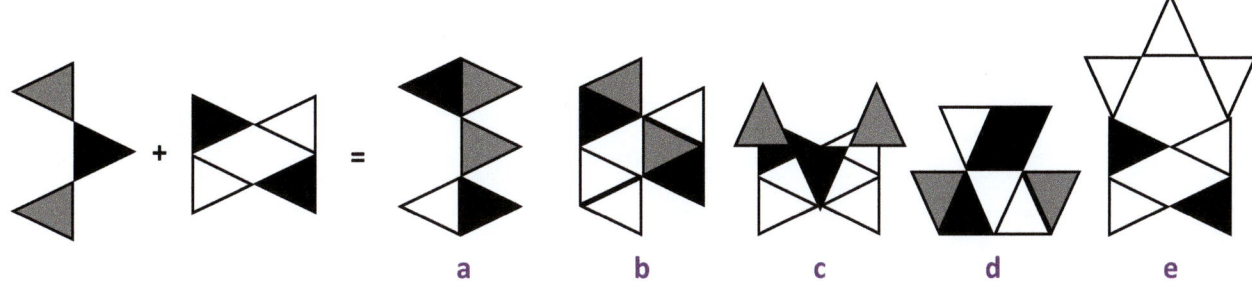

Combine the Shapes

Which shape on the right has been formed from the two shapes on the left?

9

                        a   b   c   d   e

10

                        a   b   c   d   e

Rotation Analogies

In this section, you are asked to determine the degree of rotation through which the first shape in the first pair has been rotated to form the second shape in that pair. The same degree of rotation must be applied to the second pair of shapes.

The shapes only rotate in a **clockwise** direction.

Example:

Which shape on the right has been rotated through the same number of degrees as the shape on the left?

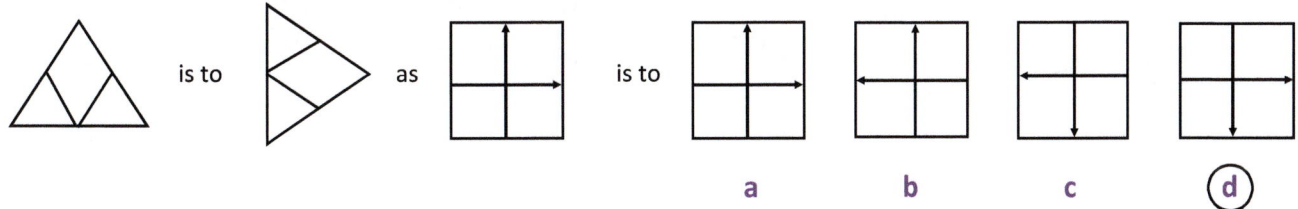

Answer: d

Explanation:

The first figure in the first pair has been rotated through 90 degrees to create the second figure.

Therefore, the first figure in the second pair must also be rotated through 90 degrees, giving figure **d**.

Rotation Analogies

Which shape on the right has been rotated through the same number of degrees as the shape on the left?

1

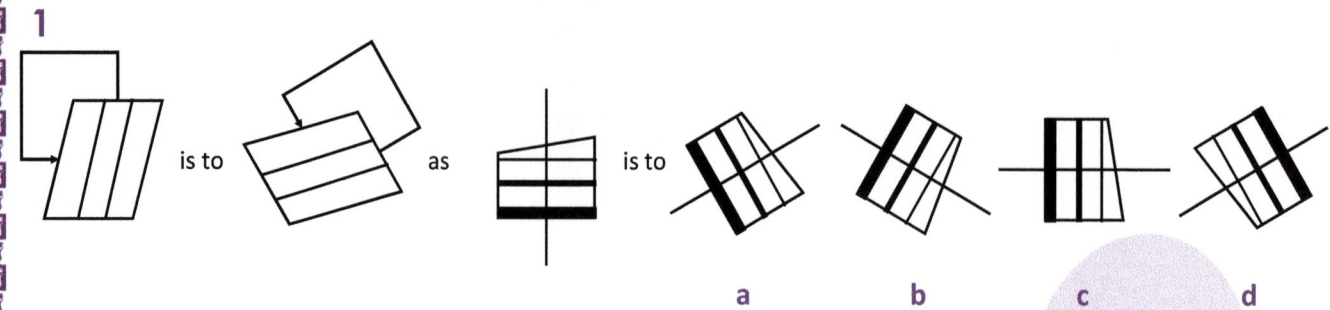

                                                                                a   b   c   d

2

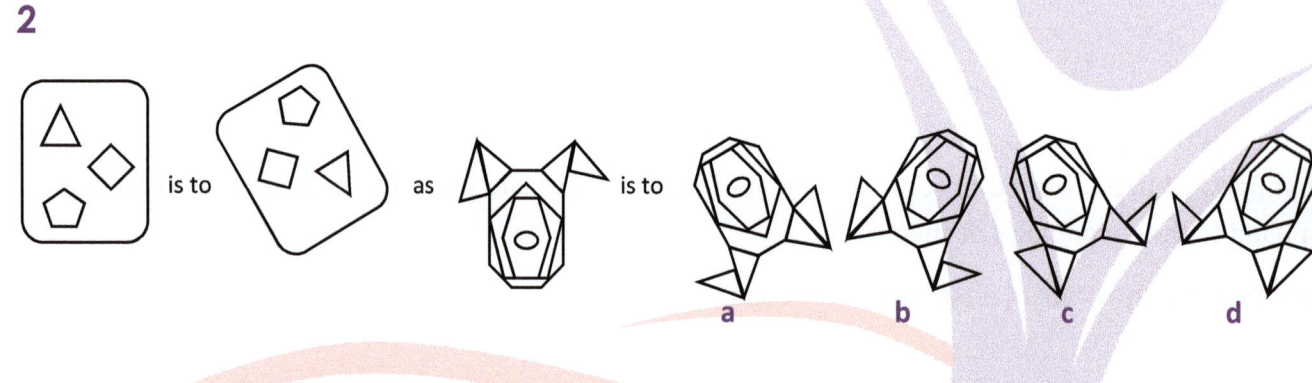

                                                                                a   b   c   d

3

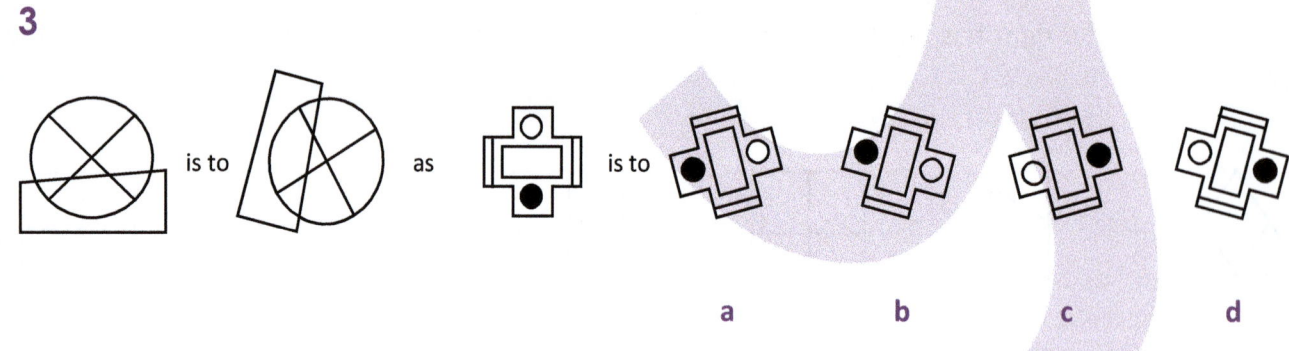

                                                                                a   b   c   d

4

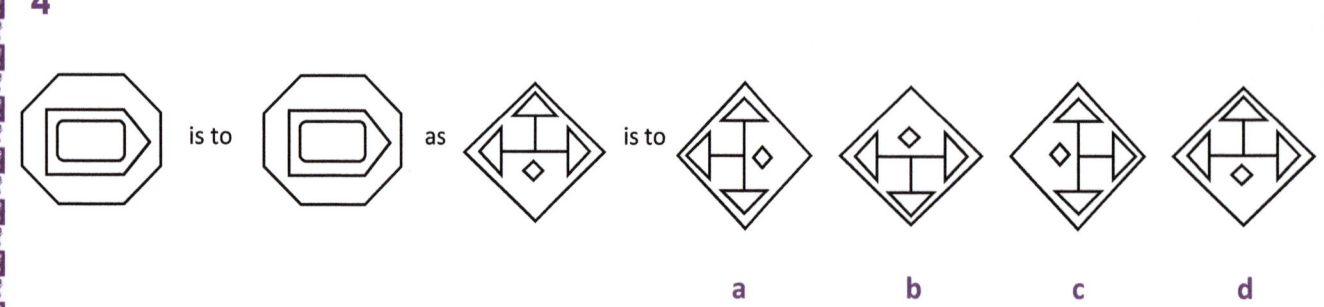

                                                                                a   b   c   d

Rotation Analogies

Which shape on the right has been rotated through the same number of degrees as the shape on the left?

5

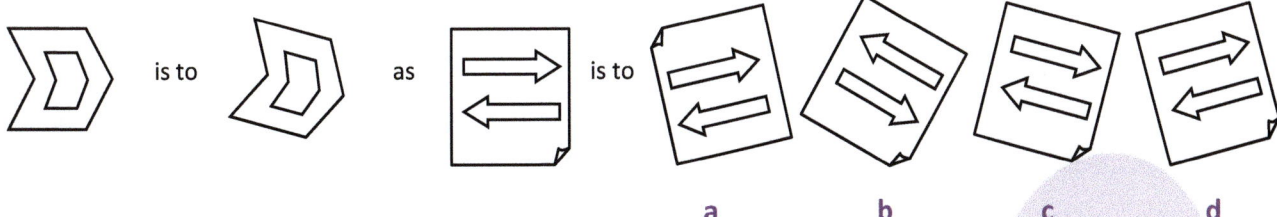

a   b   c   d

6

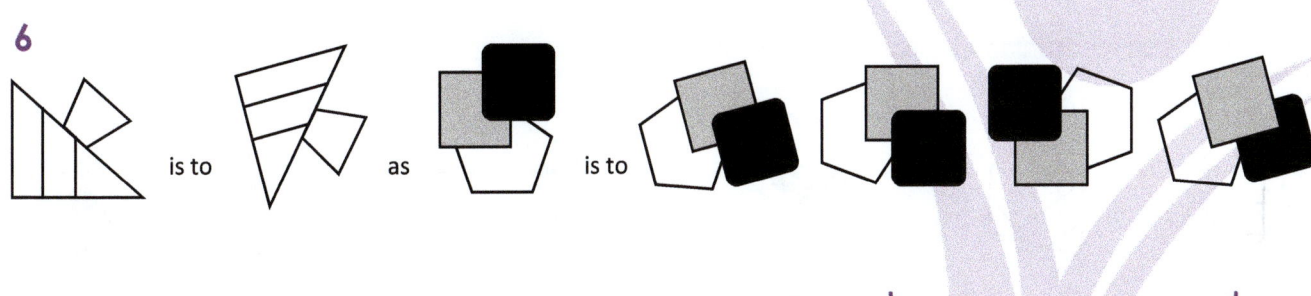

a   b   c   d

7

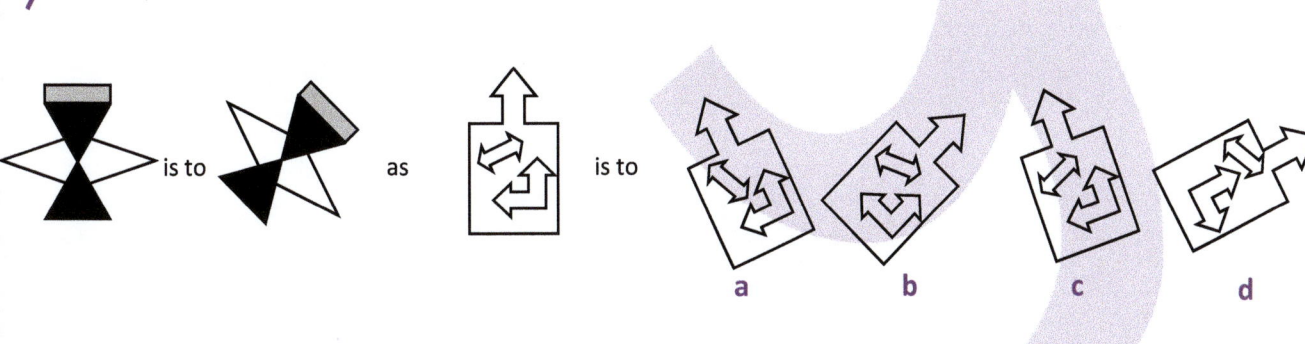

a   b   c   d

8

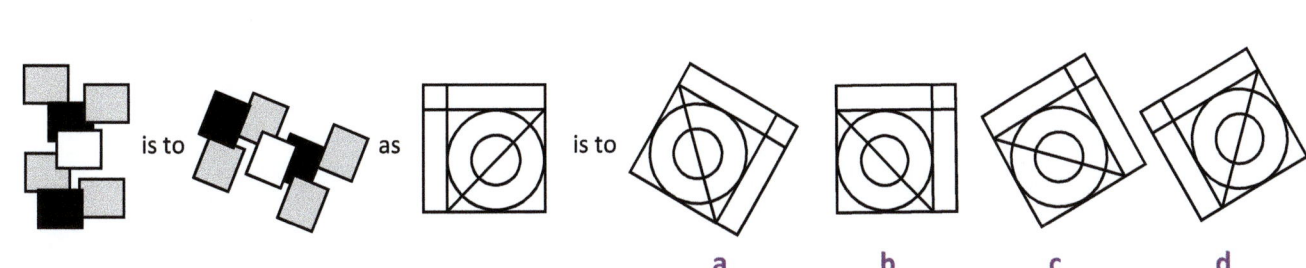

a   b   c   d

Rotation Analogies

Which shape on the right has been rotated through the same number of degrees as the shape on the left?

9

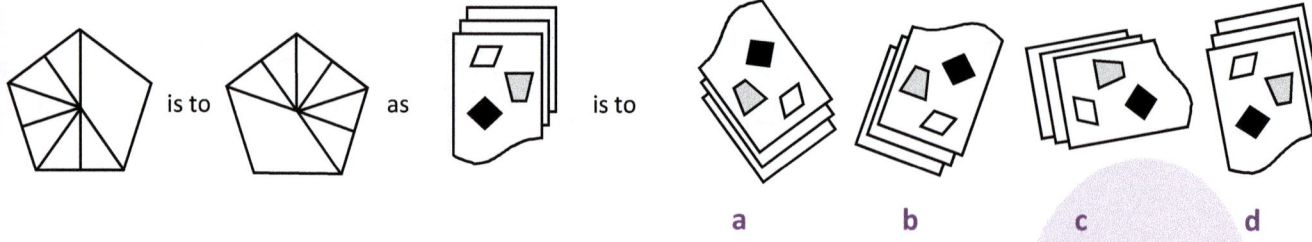

                                                      a   b   c   d

10

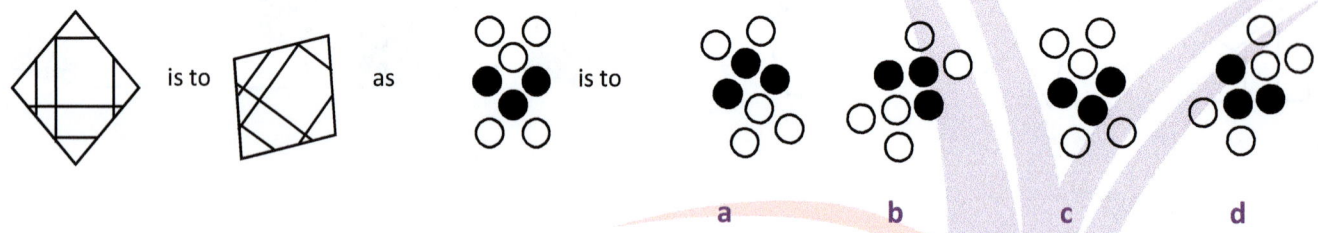

                                                      a   b   c   d

Reflection Analogies

In this section, you are asked to determine the mirror line in which the first shape in the first pair has been reflected to form the second shape in that pair. The first shape in the second pair must also be reflected in the same mirror line.

The mirror line may be horizontal, vertical or diagonal.

Example:

Which shape on the right has been reflected in the same mirror line as the shape on the left?

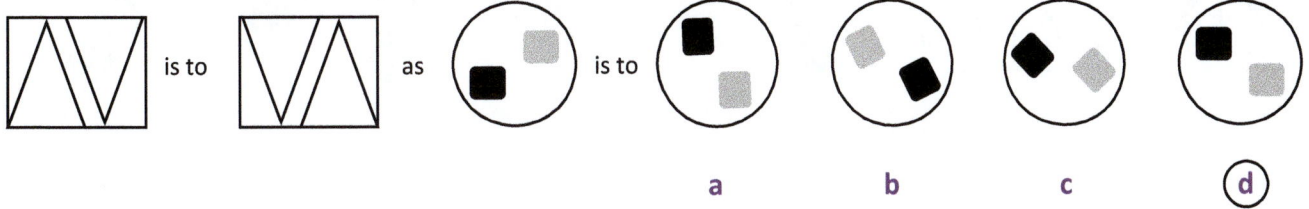

Answer: d

Explanation:

The first figure in the first pair has been reflected in an horizontal mirror line to create the second figure. Therefore, the first figure in the second pair must be reflected in an horizontal mirror line, giving figure d.

Reflection Analogies

Which shape on the right has been reflected in the same mirror line as the shape on the left?

1

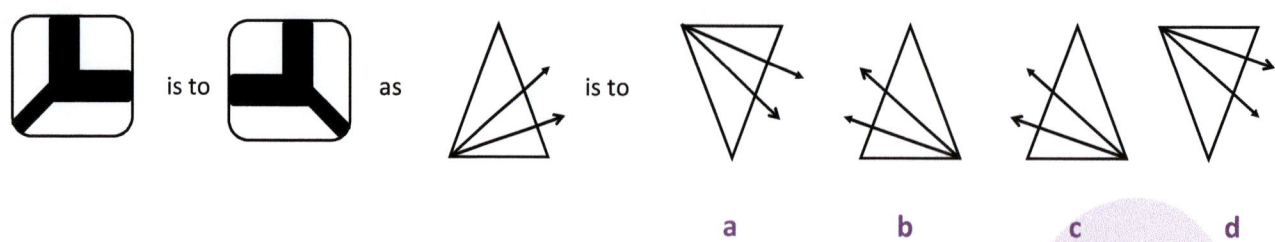

                                                        a   b   c   d

2

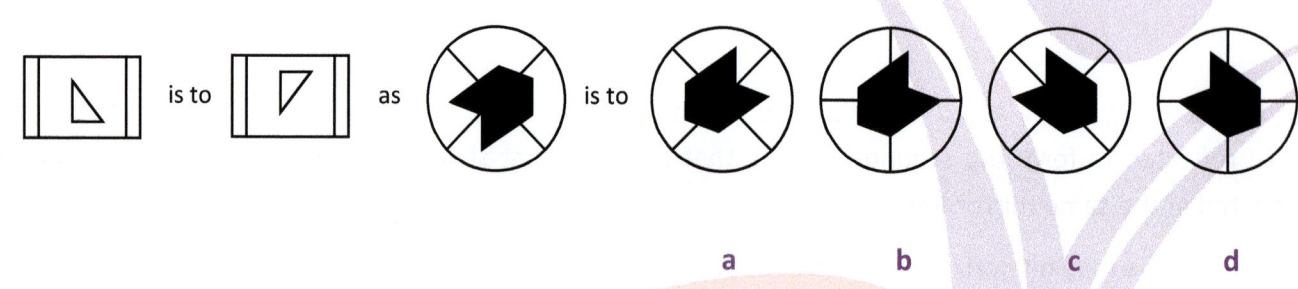

                                                        a   b   c   d

3

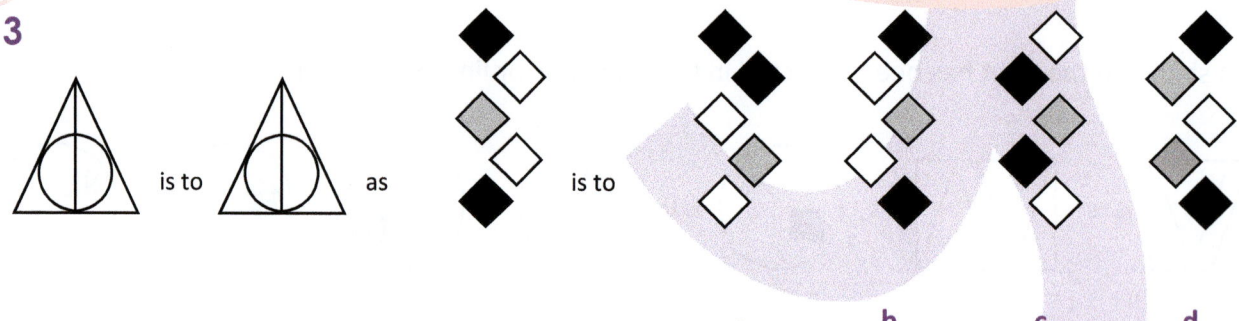

                                                        a   b   c   d

4

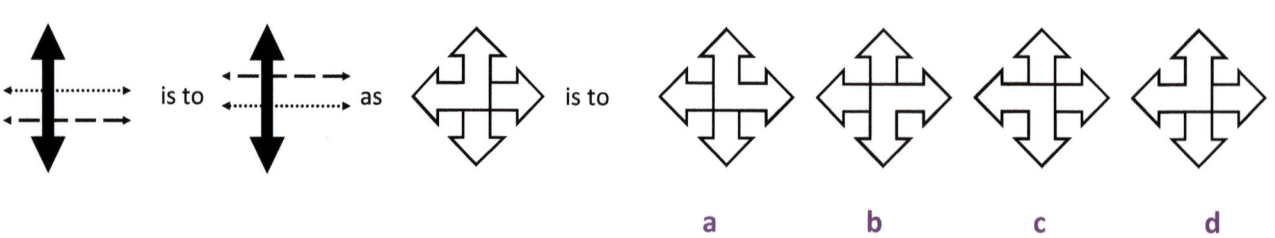

                                                        a   b   c   d

Reflection Analogies

Which shape on the right has been reflected in the same mirror line as the shape on the left?

5

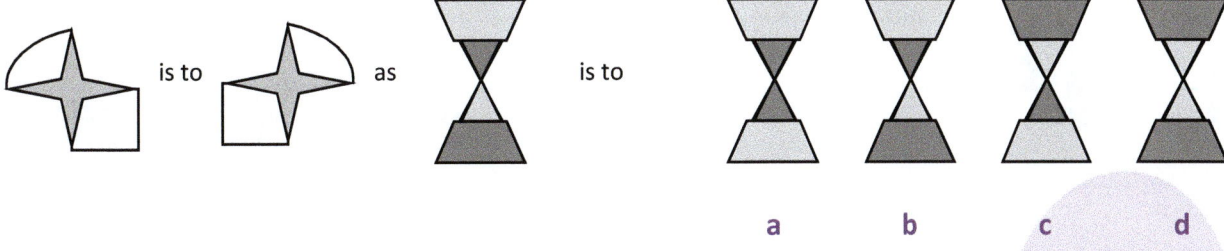

6

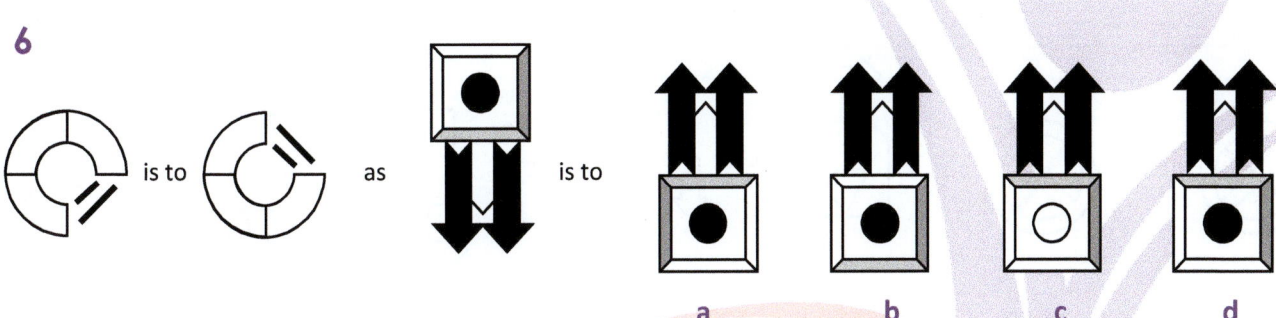

7

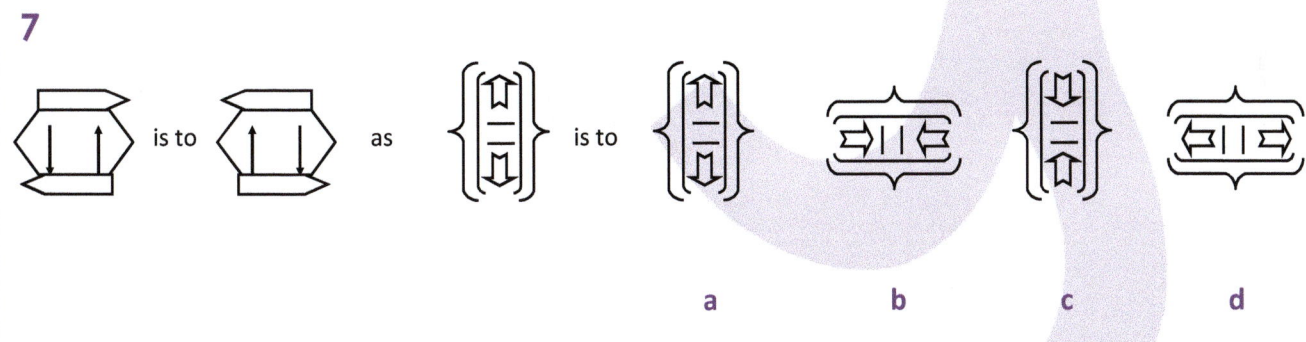

8

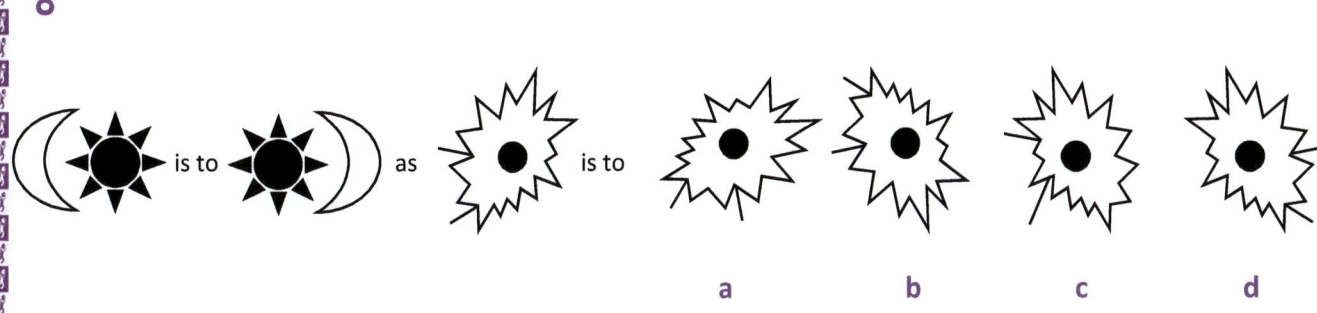

Reflection Analogies

Which shape on the right has been reflected in the same mirror line as the shape on the left?

9

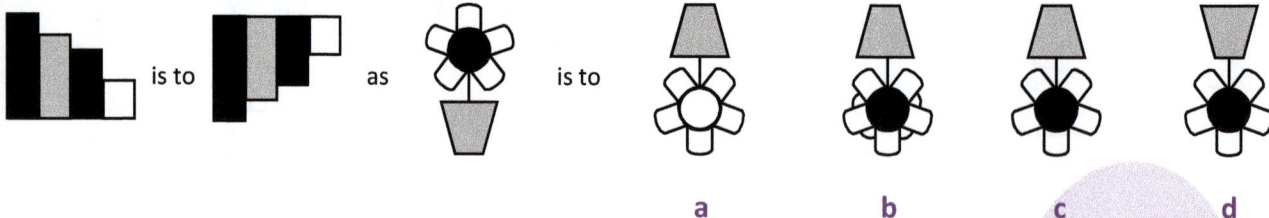

a b c d

10

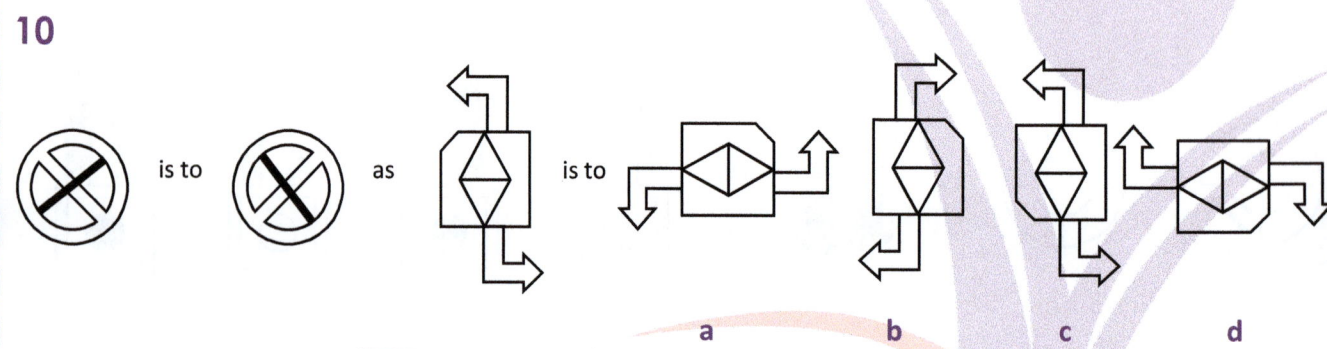

a b c d

Cross Sections

In this section, you are asked to determine which of the 2D cross sections on the right is formed when the 3D shape on the left is sliced either, horizontally or vertically, through its centre.

Straightforward questions ask the cross section of a single 3D shape, whereas more complex questions ask the cross section of a solid made up of multiple 3D shapes.

Example:

Which shape on the right is the 2D **horizontal** cross section of the centre of the 3D shape on the left?

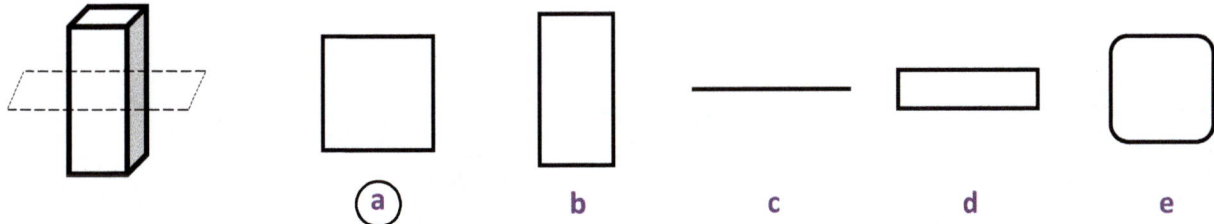

Answer: a

Explanation:

The 3D shape is a cuboid. The 2D horizontal cross section of a cuboid is either a square or rectangle. This shape has a square base, so the 2D cross section is **a**.

Cross Sections

Which shape on the right is the 2D horizontal cross section of the centre of the 3D shape on the left?

1.   a   b   c   d   e

2.   a   b   c   d   e

3.   a   b   c   d   e

4.   a   b   c   d   e

5.   a   b   c   d   e

Cross Sections

Which shape on the right is the 2D vertical cross section of the centre of the 3D shape on the left?

6

a b c d e

7

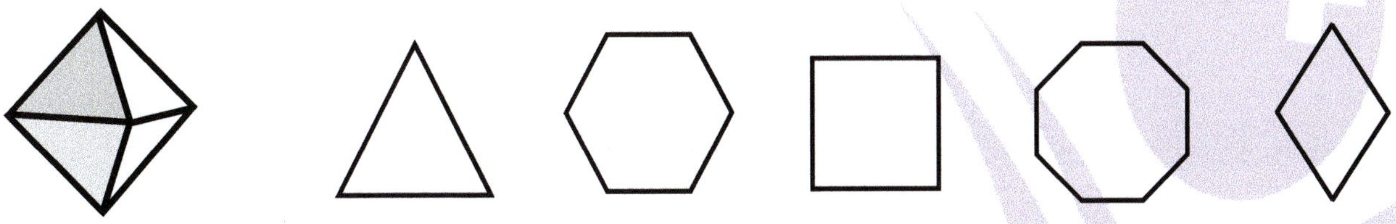

a b c d e

8

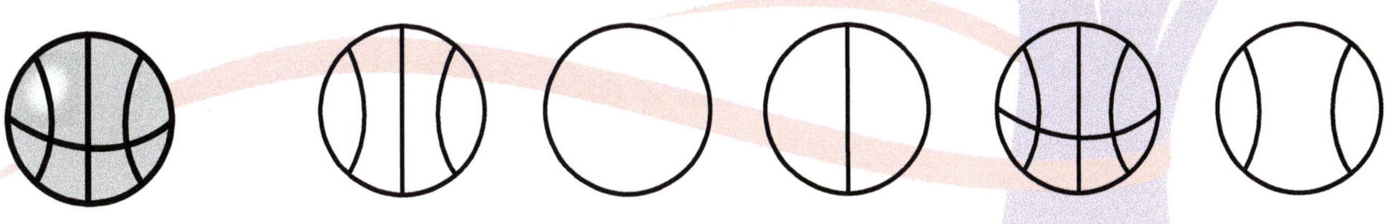

a b c d e

9

a b c d e

10

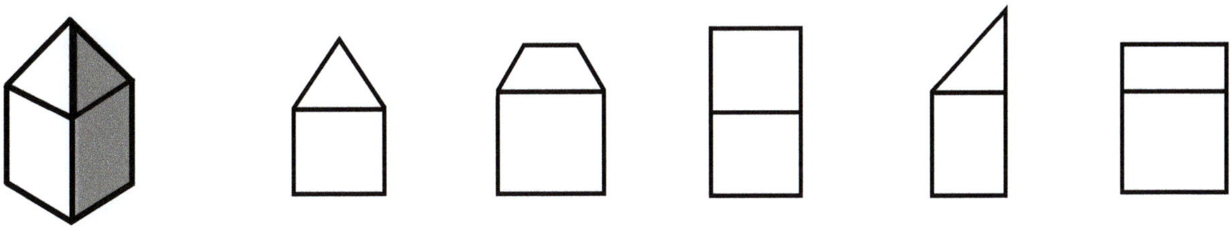

a b c d e

FIRST PAST THE POST

Answers & Explanations

Non-Verbal Reasoning:

2D

Multiple Choice

Book 2

Sequences, pages 1-4

Question	Answer	Explanation
1	d	At each step, the number of shaded circles increases by one and the arrow style alternates between dotted, dashed and solid. Therefore, the answer is **d**.
2	a	At each step, the arrow moves down one square and changes sides. In every other pattern, the circle moves down one square. Therefore, the answer is **a**.
3	d	At each step, the smaller angle between both sections of the line decreases and the number of shaded circles also decreases by one. Therefore, the answer is **d**.
4	e	At each step, the number of shaded circles decreases by one, as do the number of L-shaped lines. The L-shaped lines move around the corners of the square in a clockwise cycle and are rotated clockwise in 90 degree steps. Therefore, the answer is **e**.
5	c	The circle on the end of one of the line sections alternates between being unshaded and smaller to shaded and larger. The smaller angle between the two line sections increases at each step. The number of horizontal lines at the bottom of the vertical line increases by one at each step. Therefore, the answer is **c**.
6	c	Every other pattern in the series is rotated clockwise in 90 degree steps. Therefore, the answer is **c**.
7	e	Even-numbered patterns in the series have a shaded circle on one end of the line, whilst odd-numbered patterns in the series have two unshaded concentric circles on the end of the line. The number of points of intersection decreases by one at each step. Therefore, the answer is **e**.
8	c	The figures in the sequence alternate. Therefore, the answer is **c**.
9	d	At each step, the circle moves further down the vertical line and the shorter, vertical line moves further to the right along the horizontal line. Therefore, the answer is **d**.
10	a	At each step, the rightmost of the three vertical lines moves to the leftmost position and the remaining two lines move one place to the right. The square moves over the adjacent line to its left at each step. After the fourth pattern, the square returns to its position in the first pattern and starts its sequence again. Therefore, the answer is **a**.

Analogies, pages 5-8

Question	Answer	Explanation
1	a	The middle shape in the first figure becomes the central shape in the second figure, keeping the same border style and remaining unshaded. The central shape in the first figure becomes the outer of the two shapes in the second figure, but changes from shaded to unshaded. Therefore, the answer is **a**.
2	b	The second figure consists of all five shapes that make up the first figure, but the shapes in the second figure are placed inside each other in the same orientation as in the first figure. Therefore, the answer is **b**.
3	d	The number of thick horizontal lines and the number of smaller shapes in the second figure are the same as the number of smaller shapes in the first figure. The style of the smaller shapes is the same in both figures. Therefore, the answer is **d**.
4	b	The first figure is reflected in a vertical mirror line to give the second figure. Therefore, the answer is **b**.
5	c	The shaded sections in the first figure are unshaded in the second figure, and the unshaded sections in the first figure are shaded in the second figure. Therefore, the answer is **c**.
6	e	The first figure is reflected in an horizontal mirror line to give the second figure. Therefore, the answer is **e**.
7	b	The second figure has one fewer long lines than the first figure. The number of short lines in the second figure increases by one and the short lines are rotated 90 degrees. Therefore, the answer is **b**.
8	a	The shading pattern of the four identical shapes in the first figure is reflected in a vertical mirror line to give the shading pattern of the four identical shapes in the second figure. The shape attached to the edge flips to the opposite edge and swaps between shaded and unshaded. Therefore, the answer is **a**.
9	d	The shapes in the second figure are a smaller version of the shapes in the first figure. The shape at the bottom of the first figure swaps between shaded and unshaded. Therefore, the answer is **d**.
10	c	The first figure is rotated through 180 degrees to give the second figure. Therefore, the answer is **c**.

Codes, pages 9-12

Question	Answer	Explanation
1	d	First letter = shape style: C (two squares on left, three on right; bottom of left column is one level lower than bottom of right column), J (two squares on the left, three on the right; top of both columns at the same level), L (two squares on left, three on right; bottom of both columns at same level), N (two squares on left, two on right; bottom of right column is one level lower than bottom of left column) Second letter = shape shading: K (all squares unshaded), S (two squares shaded), Y (two squares contain dots) Shape has two squares on the left, three on the right; the bottom of both columns are at the same level, and two squares are shaded, code LS. Therefore, the answer is **d**.
2	b	First letter = number of sides on outer shape: D (4), S (5), Q (6) Second letter = number of circles: A (2), E (3), V (4), H (5) Shape consists of an outer shape with six sides containing five circles, code QH. Therefore, the answer is **b**.
3	d	First letter = number of circles: K (5), F (6), D (7), R (8) Second letter = number of shaded circles: O (1), Y (2), T (3) Shape consists of eight circles, two of which are shaded, code RY. Therefore, the answer is **d**.
4	a	First letter = number of line segments in figure (excluding square): P (5), L (8), J (11) Second letter = shape inside square: F (shaded square), S (circle), V (unshaded square), W (triangle) Shape contains 11 line segments and there is a circle inside the square, code JS. Therefore, the answer is **a**.
5	c	First letter = pattern of outer two line styles from out to in: C (dot-dashed, solid), N (solid, dot-dashed), Z (dashed, solid) Second letter = central shape: G (square), K (hexagon), O (curved shape), T (circle) Shape has outer line styles of dashed and solid, and has a hexagon at its centre, code ZK. Therefore, the answer is **c**.
6	e	First letter = circle positions: M (touching inside sides of the shape), O (touching outside corners of the shape), S (touching outside sides of the shape) Second letter = direction of U-like shape: R (sideways like a 'c'), T (upward like a 'u'), U (downward like an 'n') Shape consists of two circles touching the outside corners of the n-like shape, code OU. Therefore, the answer is **e**.
7	a	First letter = direction in which triangle is pointing: L (left), T (up), Y (right) Second letter = number of shaded circles: O (1), B (2), D (3) Shape has a triangle pointing left and three shaded circles, code LD. Therefore, the answer is **a**.
8	d	First letter = circle position: A (circle underneath square), C (circle right of square), J (circle above square) Second letter = square shading: D (half the square shaded), F (whole square shaded), Q (quarter of the square shaded) Shape consists of a circle above the square and half the square is shaded, code JD. Therefore, the answer is **d**.
9	b	First letter = shape style: A (hexagon), B (triangle), C (circle) Second letter = number of lines intersecting the sides of the shape: K (1), M (2), N (3) Shape is a triangle with two lines intersecting its sides, code BM. Therefore, the answer is **b**.
10	e	First letter = shape orientation: I (vertical), J (slanting), K (horizontal) Second letter = shading style: X (light grey), Y (unshaded), Z (dark grey) Third letter = number of stars: A (0), B (1), C (2) Shape is slanting, has dark grey shading and has two stars, code JZC. Therefore, the answer is **e**.

Similarities, pages 13-16

Question	Answer	Explanation
1	c	The ratio of unshaded to shaded sections within each shape is 3:1. Therefore, the answer is **c**.
2	a	Each figure consists of two or more parallel lines and one line which is perpendicular to the parallel lines. There is always only one shaded or unshaded circle sitting on the right of the first parallel line. Therefore, the answer is **a**.
3	d	If the larger shape has a solid outline, then one rectangle is on top of it. If the larger shape has a dotted outline, then two rectangles are on top of it. If the larger shape has a thicker outline, then the rectangle(s) are unshaded. If the larger shape has a thinner outline, then the rectangle(s) are shaded. Therefore, the answer is **d**.
4	e	Each figure consists of a kite, rectangle, triangle, circle and square, which are arranged one above the other in a vertical line and appear in any order. The shapes alternate between interlinking and touching each other. The top shape is always shaded and the others are always unshaded. Therefore, the answer is **e**.
5	a	Three identical parallel lines touch each side of the larger shape and either point into or away from the shape. The outline of the larger shape must be solid. Therefore, the answer is **a**.
6	c	Each figure consists of a longer line and a shorter line which are perpendicular to each other. The shapes on the ends of each line are identical in style and in shading. Therefore, the answer is **c**.
7	a	Each figure shows a shape with one dashed line through its centre. The dashed line is a line of symmetry. Therefore, the answer is **a**.
8	b	Each figure consists of three larger unshaded shapes which are arranged on top of each other with their edges touching. The middle of the three unshaded shapes is always a triangle which always points upwards. The top and bottom of the three unshaded shapes are different. The top unshaded shape contains a smaller shaded version of the unshaded shape at the bottom and vice versa. Therefore, the answer is **b**.
9	c	Each figure consists of the letter 'H' in a different style. The style of the two parallel sides are always the same, while the style of the shorter perpendicular side is always different. Therefore, the answer is **c**.
10	b	Each shape consists of a long, curved line with a number of shorter, straight lines crossing each other at one of the ends. The number of shorter, straight lines at the end of the longer, curved lines is the same as the number of shorter lines that cross through the middle of the longer, curved line. Therefore, the answer is **b**.

Odd One Out, pages 17-20

Question	Answer	Explanation
1	c	In all figures but **c**, the number of diamonds in the bottom square is half the number of diamonds in the top square.
2	e	In all figures but **e**, opposite sides with a solid or dotted line next to them are of equal length.
3	b	In all figures but **b**, the shading is horizontal.
4	e	In all figures but **e**, shapes with the same shading pattern are found on only one side of the wavy line.
5	b	In all figures but **b**, there is a minimum of two shaded circles on both sides of the line that cuts across the shape.
6	d	In all figures but **d**, the number of small circles is one more than the number of sides of the shape on the left.
7	d	In all figures but **d**, the smaller of the two shapes has been rotated anticlockwise by 90 degrees.
8	b	In all figures but **b**, the dashed line is a line of symmetry.
9	d	In all figures but **d**, the inner polygon is an horizontally mirrored, smaller version of the larger, outer shape.
10	c	In all figures but **c**, the shaded triangle(s) point upwards.

Complete the Square Grid, pages 21-24

Question	Answer	Explanation
1	c	The shapes in each column are identical in style but move from the top left corner, to the middle, to the bottom right corner of each square. The number of shaded sections of each shape is equal to the number of short vertical lines in the top right corner of each square. In the rightmost and leftmost columns, the shaded sections increase going down the column. In the middle column, the shaded sections decrease going down the column. Therefore, the answer is **c**.
2	d	The figure styles in each row are identical, but there are two arrows in the second column and one arrow in the first column. In each row, one of the two arrows in the second column is missing in the first column. Therefore, the answer is **d**.
3	a	Across each row, the line on the far left in each square moves to the far right of the next square, and the other lines move one position to the left. If the line has a shape above it, the shape moves with the line. Therefore, the answer is **a**.
4	e	Across each row, the figure in the square is rotated 180 degrees with identical shapes alternating between shaded and unshaded. Therefore, answer is **e**.
5	c	In the middle column, longer lines are both dotted. Across each row, the indicated angle between the two longer lines increases in approximately 45 degree steps. The number of shorter lines on the ends of the two longer lines increases by two across the rows and down the columns. Therefore, the answer is **c**.
6	b	The shape in the third row is identical to the shape in the first row of that column. Therefore, the answer is **b**.
7	e	Each square contains a rectangle and a kite which exchange positions across the row. The number of shaded circles within the rectangle increases by two across each row. The number of shaded circles within the rectangle is equal to the number of grey sections within the kite. The kite always has the same orientation. Therefore, the answer is **e**.
8	e	The shapes in each row are the same, but have been rotated anticlockwise in 90 degree steps. One shape in each column is shaded and two are unshaded. In the first column, the middle shape is shaded. In the second column, the outermost shape is shaded, and in the third column the innermost shape is shaded. Therefore, the answer is **e**.
9	a	The figures in the first column are smaller, identical versions of the figures in the second column, with the same orientation. Shapes in the first column are unshaded and shapes in the second column are shaded. Therefore, the answer is **a**.
10	d	Across each row, the shaded shape moves from the bottom, to the middle, to the top of each square. Across each row, the line on the left of each square moves further down and decreases in length, while the line on the right of each square moves further up and decreases in length. Therefore, the answer is **d**.

Complete the Grid, pages 25-28

Question	Answer	Explanation
1	b	Moving in a clockwise direction from the top, left hexagon, the number of sides on the shape within the hexagon increases by one, and the number of short lines inside each shape also increases by one. Therefore, the answer is **b**.
2	b	The shapes in diagonally opposite crosses are identical in style and position. Therefore, the answer is **b**.
3	c	Moving in a clockwise direction from the top hexagon, the number of parallel lines is equal to the number of sides on the shaded shape in the next hexagon. Therefore, the answer is **c**.
4	d	Moving in a clockwise direction from the right octagon, the arrow rotates 45 degrees clockwise at each stage. Moving in an anticlockwise direction from the right octagon, the number of short lines doubles at each stage. Therefore, the answer is **d**.
5	c	For hexagons directly opposite each other, the number of lines touching the sides of the hexagon is equal to the number of sections within the rectangle inside the opposite hexagon. Therefore, the answer is **c**.
6	b	The bottom three hexagons are a reflection in an horizontal line of the top three hexagons. Therefore, the answer is **b**.
7	c	The number of sections within each trapezium is equal to the number of sides of the adjacent shape inside the central square. The number of stars inside each of these shapes is equal to the number of shaded sections in the adjacent trapezium. Therefore, the answer is **c**.
8	d	The shapes within the hexagons directly opposite each other are identical in style, but have been rotated through 180 degrees. The style of the arrowhead in adjacent hexagons alternates. Therefore, the answer is **d**.
9	d	Moving in a clockwise direction from the top, right cross, the circle moves around the sides in a clockwise cycle. The small cross moves around the corners in a clockwise cycle. The line section without an arrowhead rotates 90 degrees clockwise at each stage. Therefore, the answer is **d**.
10	a	The shapes within the hexagons directly opposite each other are identical in style, but have been rotated through 180 degrees. Moving in an anticlockwise direction from the bottom, right hexagon, the number of crosses increases by one at each stage. Therefore, the answer is **a**.

Reflections, pages 29-32

Question	Answer	Explanation
1	c	Although options a and c show the required reflection, in option a, the parallelogram is incorrectly oriented. Therefore, the answer is **c**.
2	a	Although options a and d show the required reflection, in option d, the shaded circle is in the wrong position. Therefore, the answer is **a**.
3	b	The triangle is pointing to the right in the original figure, so it will be pointing to the left in the reflection. Therefore, the answer is **b**.
4	c	Three of the four lines in the original shape are left-leaning and will therefore be right-leaning in the reflection. Although options a and c have three right-leaning lines, only option c shows all the lines reflected at the correct angles. Therefore, the answer is **c**.
5	b	As the right side of the square is a dashed line in the original figure, the left side of the reflection will be a dashed line, as in options a, b and d. In the reflection, the shape inside the square will be close to the dashed line and pointing to the right. Therefore, the answer is **b**.
6	c	In the reflection, the vertical line will be closest to the mirror line, and the three right-pointing horizontal lines of the original figure will remain horizontal, but point to the left. Therefore, the answer is **c**.
7	b	The left-leaning shape will appear right-leaning in the reflection, as in options a, b and d. The end of the line will be at the bottom of the shape. Therefore, the answer is **b**.
8	b	The small, unshaded square will appear in the bottom, left-hand corner of the reflection, and the larger, shaded square will appear in the top, right-hand corner of the reflection. Therefore, the answer is **b**.
9	c	The slanted, top, left-hand corner of the large square will appear in the top, right-hand corner of the reflection, as in answers b and c. The right-leaning diagonal line inside the small square will appear left-leaning in the reflection. Therefore, the answer is **c**.
10	b	All arrows in the reflection must face in the opposite direction to those in the original figure. Therefore, the answer is **b**.

Rotations, pages 33-36

Question	Answer	Explanation
1	b	Option a: The shaded square is in the wrong place. Option c: The right-angled triangle is flipped over. Option d: The isosceles triangle is pointing towards the line instead of away from it. Option **b**: Correct clockwise rotation through 135 degrees.
2	a	Option b: The shaded parallelogram is slanting towards the cross instead of away from it. Option c: This is the mirror image of the original figure. Option d: There are two arrowheads on the inner L-shape. Option **a**: Correct anticlockwise rotation through an acute angle.
3	c	Option a: The outer shape is flipped. Option b: The two centre circles have swapped places. Option d: The circles are too far to the right of the outer shape. Option **c**: Correct clockwise rotation through an obtuse angle.
4	d	Option a: The arrow and star have swapped places. Option b: The three edges sticking out of the outer shape are sticking inwards. Option c: The arrow is pointing away from the centre of the shape instead of towards it. Option **d**: Correct clockwise rotation through 135 degrees.
5	a	Option b: An extra line has been added. Option c: The inner circle and its contents have moved to the centre of the outer circle. Option d: The shaded oval has moved to the other side of the hexagon. Option **a**: Correct rotation through 180 degrees.
6	b	Option a: The unshaded square and grey-shaded triangle have swapped places. Option c: The unshaded square has changed to a dark-shaded square. Option d: This is the mirror image of the original figure. Option **b**: Correct anticlockwise rotation through an obtuse angle.
7	b	Option a: The shaded rectangles are incorrectly oriented. Option c: The position of the short line has moved to the opposite side of the octagon. Option d: The trapezium has been replaced by a rectangle. Option **b**: Correct clockwise rotation through 45 degrees.
8	d	Option a: The wavy line is flipped over. Option b: The tick is flipped over. Option c: This is the mirror image of the original figure rotated 45 degrees clockwise. Option **d**: Correct rotation through 360 degrees.
9	c	Option a: The parallelogram is flipped over. Option b: The triangle is unshaded. Option d: The curved line and parallelogram are flipped over. Option **c**: Correct clockwise rotation through 135 degrees.
10	a	Option b: One line is missing from the right-hand side of the figure. Option c: The position of the unshaded circle has changed. Option d: The diagonal line is slanting the wrong way. Option **a**: Correct rotation through 180 degrees.

Hidden Shapes, pages 37-40

Question	Answer	Explanation
1	e	The target shape consists of two overlapping, differently sized circles. Options b and c show overlapping circles of the same size, and the overlapping circles in option a are too large. Option d contains no overlapping circles. Option e contains an exact replica of the target shape, but rotated through 180 degrees. Therefore, the answer is **e**.
2	b	Options a, c and d all contain shapes that resemble the target shape. In option b, however, an exact replica of the target shape can be seen in the top, left corner of the figure, having been rotated anticlockwise by 90 degrees. Therefore, the answer is **b**.
3	d	Options a, b, c and e all contain shapes that resemble the target shape, but with minor changes. An exact replica of the target shape can be seen in the bottom, right corner of option d. Therefore, the answer is **d**.
4	b	A shape loosely resembling the target shape appears in options a, c, d and e. The target shape only occurs exactly in option b, but at 90 degrees to the original. Therefore, the answer is **b**.
5	e	Options a, b, c and d show examples of a circle with lines inside, but none with two lines at 90 degrees to each other and joining at the centre of the circle. This can only be seen in option e, where an enlarged replica of the target shape is present. Therefore, the answer is **e**.
6	c	An exact replica of the target shape appears in the bottom two rows of option c. Therefore, the answer is **c**.
7	e	The angle between the two lines in the target shape is an important element to look for in the options available. It is only in option **e**, along the left leaning line, that his angle is apparent, even though the shape is shown after a 180 degree rotation. Therefore, the answer is **e**.
8	a	Although a shape similar to the target shape can be seen in option b, its proportions are not the same. An enlarged, reflected image of the target shape is shown in option a. Therefore, the answer is **a**.
9	e	The only place where three short lines are attached at the correct angles and at the correct distances apart to a longer line is on the right-leaning line of the triangle in option e. Therefore, the answer is **e**.
10	c	The target shape consists of three concentric circles, with the central one shaded. Although options b and e contain an oval version of this shape, only option c shows an exact replica of the target shape. Therefore, the answer is **c**.

Identify the Pair, pages 41-44

Question	Answer	Explanation
1	**b & d**	Option c can be eliminated because the dashed octagon is missing. Option e can be eliminated because the central circle is unshaded. Option a can be eliminated because the hexagon is incorrectly oriented. This leaves options **b & d** as the pair.
2	**a & c**	Option d can be eliminated because the circle closest to the curved arrow is shaded. Option e can be eliminated because the curved arrow is pointing in the wrong direction. Option b can be eliminated because the jagged line has the wrong pattern. This leaves options **a & c** as the pair.
3	**b & e**	Option c can be eliminated because the thick, black cross is in the wrong place. Option a can be eliminated because the finely dotted line has become dashed. Option d can be eliminated because the shaded circle is too close to the horizontal, thick, black line. This leaves options **b & e** as the pair.
4	**a & d**	Option b can be eliminated because the shaded circle is incorrectly positioned at the end of the rectangle. Option c can be eliminated because there are four, instead of three, dashes in the rectangle. Option e can be eliminated because the smaller, shaded circle inside the unshaded circle is on the left, instead of on the right. This leaves options **a & d** as the pair.
5	**c & e**	Option a can be eliminated because the parallelogram is too big. Option d can be eliminated because the wavy lines are too thin. Option b can be eliminated because the pentagon has been changed to a square. This leaves options **c & e** as the pair.
6	**c & e**	Option a can be eliminated because the cross is too big. Option d can be eliminated because the shading pattern of the small ovals is reversed. Option b can be eliminated because the large, white ovals are incorrectly oriented. This leaves options **c & e** as the pair.
7	**a & b**	Option d can be eliminated because the wavy lines are incorrectly oriented. Option e can be eliminated because there is a dotted, instead of a dashed, line in the small rectangle. Option c can be eliminated because the black, curved shape is slanting in the wrong direction. This leaves options **a & b** as the pair.
8	**a & d**	Option c can be eliminated because the black and white circles have swapped sides. Option e can be eliminated because there is a dashed, instead of a dotted, line. Option b can be eliminated because the diagonal line in the small rectangle is slanting the wrong way. This leaves options **a & d** as the pair.
9	**d & e**	Option b can be eliminated because there are only two diagonal lines in the top section of the treble clef, instead of three. Option a can be eliminated because two of the black dots in the bass clef have been swapped round. Option c can be eliminated because the curved arrow is pointing up instead of down. This leaves options **d & e** as the pair.
10	**b & d**	Option e can be eliminated because the smiley face is too far to the right. Option a can be eliminated because there is a line inside the small triangle on the right. Option c can be eliminated because the small, black dot at the bottom of the central, vertical line is on the wrong side of it. This leaves options **b & d** as the pair.

Combine the Shapes, pages 45-48

Question	Answer	Explanation
1	a	If the first shape is rotated 135 degrees anticlockwise and the second shape is rotated 90 degrees anticlockwise, the resulting shapes can be placed on top of each other to give option **a**.
2	e	The second shape can be reflected in a vertical mirror line and placed on top of the first shape to give option **e**.
3	d	If the two shapes are placed next to each other, the resulting shape can be rotated through 180 degrees to give option **d**.
4	c	The first shape can be placed on top of the right side of the second shape to give option **c**.
5	b	If the second shape is rotated 90 degrees and the first shape is rotated 180 degrees, the resulting shapes can be vertically aligned to give option **b**.
6	d	If the first shape is connected to the right side of the second shape, the resulting shape can be rotated 135 degrees clockwise to give option **d**.
7	e	If the first shape is transparent and is placed on top of the second shape, the resulting shape can be rotated 90 degrees anticlockwise to give option **e**.
8	d	If the second shape is transparent and is placed on top of the first shape, the resulting shape can be rotated 90 degrees anticlockwise to give option **d**.
9	b	If the first shape is rotated 90 degrees clockwise and the second shape is rotated 45 degrees clockwise, the resulting shapes can be placed on top of each other to give option **b**.
10	c	If the second shape is transparent and the first shape is rotated 90 degrees, the second shape can be placed over the centre of the first shape to give option **c**.

© 2018 ElevenPlusExams.co.uk COPYING STRICTLY PROHIBITED

Rotation Analogies, pages 49-52

Question	Answer	Explanation
1	a	The first figure in the first pair has been rotated 60 degrees to create the second figure. Therefore, when the first figure in the second pair is rotated 60 degrees, it creates figure **a**.
2	a	The first figure in the first pair has been rotated 150 degrees to create the second figure. Therefore, when the first figure in the second pair is rotated 150 degrees, it creates figure **a**.
3	b	The first figure in the first pair has been rotated 105 degrees to create the second figure. Therefore, when the first figure in the second pair is rotated 105 degrees, it creates figure **b**.
4	d	The first figure in the first pair has been rotated 360 degrees to create the second figure. Therefore, when the first figure in the second pair is rotated 360 degrees, it creates figure **d**.
5	c	The first figure in the first pair has been rotated 15 degrees to create the second figure. Therefore, when the first figure in the second pair is rotated 15 degrees, it creates figure **c**.
6	a	The first figure in the first pair has been rotated 75 degrees to create the second figure. Therefore, when the first figure in the second pair is rotated 75 degrees, it creates figure **a**.
7	b	The first figure in the first pair has been rotated 45 degrees to create the second figure. Therefore, when the first figure in the second pair is rotated 45 degrees, it creates figure **b**.
8	a	The first figure in the first pair has been rotated 120 degrees to create the second figure. Therefore, when the first figure in the second pair is rotated 120 degrees, it creates figure **a**.
9	a	The first figure in the first pair has been rotated 145 degrees to create the second figure. Therefore, when the first figure in the second pair is rotated 145 degrees, it creates figure **a**.
10	d	The first figure in the first pair has been rotated 35 degrees to create the second figure. Therefore, when the first figure in the second pair is rotated 35 degrees, it creates figure **d**.

Reflection Analogies, pages 53-56

Question	Answer	Explanation
1	c	The first figure in the first pair has been reflected in a vertical mirror line to create the second figure. Therefore, when the first figure in the second pair is reflected in a vertical mirror line, it creates figure **c**.
2	c	The first figure in the first pair has been reflected in an horizontal mirror line to create the second figure. Therefore, when the first figure in the second pair is reflected in a horizontal mirror line, it creates figure **c**.
3	b	The first figure in the first pair has been reflected in a vertical mirror line to create the second figure. Therefore, when the first figure in the second pair is reflected in a vertical mirror line, it creates figure **b**.
4	c	The first figure in the first pair has been reflected in an horizontal mirror line to create the second figure. Therefore, when the first figure in the second pair is reflected in a horizontal mirror line, it creates figure **c**.
5	b	The first figure in the first pair has been reflected in a vertical mirror line to create the second figure. Therefore, when the first figure in the second pair is reflected in a vertical mirror line, it creates figure **b**.
6	d	The first figure in the first pair has been reflected in an horizontal mirror line to create the second figure. Therefore, when the first figure in the second pair is reflected in a horizontal mirror line, it creates figure **d**.
7	a	The first figure in the first pair has been reflected in a vertical mirror line to create the second figure. Therefore, when the first figure in the second pair is reflected in a vertical mirror line, it creates figure **a**.
8	d	The first figure in the first pair has been reflected in a vertical mirror line to create the second figure. Therefore, when the first figure in the second pair is reflected in a vertical mirror line, it creates figure **d**.
9	c	The first figure in the first pair has been reflected in an horizontal mirror line to create the second figure. Therefore, when the first figure in the second pair is reflected in a horizontal mirror line, it creates figure **c**.
10	b	The first figure in the first pair has been reflected in a vertical mirror line to create the second figure. Therefore, when the first figure in the second pair is reflected in a vertical mirror line, it creates figure **b**.

Cross Sections, pages 57-60

Question	Answer	Explanation
1	b	The 3D shape is made up of two cuboids. As the sliced plane is parallel to the base, the 2D horizontal cross section will be the same as the base, which is a rectangle. Therefore, the answer is **b**.
2	a	The 3D shape is a sphere. All cross sections of a sphere are circles, therefore the 2D horizontal cross section is a circle. Therefore, the answer is **a**.
3	c	The 3D shape is a square-based pyramid. As the sliced plane is parallel to the base, the 2D horizontal cross section will be the same as the base, which is a square. Therefore, the answer is **c**.
4	a	The 3D shape is made up of multiple adjacent cylinders, creating an upside-down 'V' shape. As the sliced plane is parallel to the base, the 2D horizontal cross section will be the same as the base, which is a series of circles. However, the second and fourth cylinders are hollow, so their cross sections will have a hole in the middle. Therefore, the answer is **a**.
5	c	The 3D shape is made up of two cuboids and a plus-shaped solid. For the cuboids, as the sliced plane is parallel to the base, the 2D horizontal cross section will be the same as the base, which is a square. The sliced plane will pass through the horizontal cuboid of the plus-shaped solid, so the 2D horizontal cross section will be a rectangle. As there are gaps between the three shapes, there will also be gaps between their cross sections. Thus, the 2D horizontal cross section will be two squares and a rectangle with gaps in between. Therefore, the answer is **a**.
6	b	The 3D shape is a tetrahedron. The diagrams on the right show how the 2D vertical cross section is formed. Therefore, the answer is **b**.
7	e	The 3D shape is an octahedron. The diagrams on the right show how the 2D vertical cross section is formed. Therefore, the answer is **e**.
8	b	The 3D shape resembles a basketball. A basketball is a sphere with markings on the outside. Therefore, the 2D vertical cross section will be that of a sphere, which is a circle. As the markings are on the outside, they will not be seen on the cross section. Therefore, the answer is **b**.
9	a	The 3D shape is made up of three cylinders stacked on top of each other. The vertical cross section of a cylinder is a rectangle, so the 2D vertical cross section of the solid will be three rectangles of decreasing widths directly on top of each other. Therefore, the answer is **a**.
10	a	The 3D solid is made up of a cuboid and a square-based pyramid. The 2D vertical cross section of a square-based pyramid is a triangle. The 2D vertical cross section of a cuboid is a rectangle. Therefore, the 2D vertical cross section will be a triangle on top of a rectangle. Therefore, the answer is **a**.

Other Titles in the First Past The Post® Series

Non-Verbal Reasoning: 2D

These books focus on developing the candidate's visuospatial and pattern-identification skills with two-dimensional shapes. Each book provides topic-specific practice, with 15 chapters covering all known question styles likely to come up in 2D Non-Verbal Reasoning 11 plus and Common Entrance exams. Full answers and explanations are included.

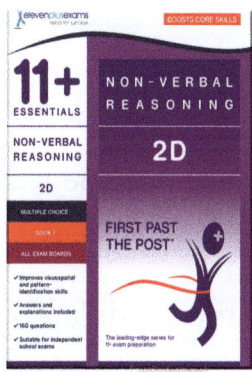

Each book contains 15 topic-specific chapters, each focusing on one of the following: sequences, analogies, codes, similarities, odd one out, complete the square grid, complete the grid, reflections, rotations, hidden shapes, identify the pair, combine the shapes, rotation analogies, reflection analogies and cross sections.

Other Titles in the First Past The Post® Series

Non-Verbal Reasoning: 3D

These books focus on developing the candidate's visuospatial and pattern-identification skills with three-dimensional shapes. Each book contains four topic-specific chapters, each focusing on one of 3D views, 3D composite shapes, 3D cube nets and 3D plan views, and four mixed tests. The mixed tests have been designed to provide real exam practice under a time pressure representative of that in the real exam. Full answers are included.

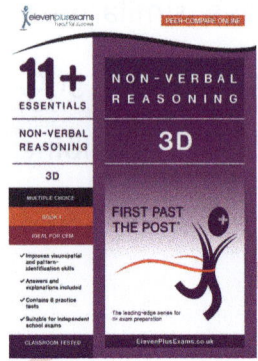

Each test can be marked and evaluated via our Peer-Compare™ Online system, which assesses the candidate's performance anonymously on a question-by-question basis. This helps identify areas for improvement and benchmarks the candidate's score against that of others who have taken the same tests.

Other Titles in the First Past The Post® Series

Non-Verbal Reasoning: Practice Papers (GL)

These books provide real exam practice via four timed tests. These are tailored towards the Granada Learning (GL) Non-Verbal Reasoning assessments but provide invaluable practice for all exam boards. Each test covers a range of 2D question styles, reflecting the likely make-up of the real exam. Full answers and explanations are included.

Each test can be marked and evaluated via our Peer-Compare™ Online system, which assesses the candidate's performance anonymously on a question-by-question basis. This helps identify areas for improvement and benchmarks the candidate's score against that of others who have taken the same tests.

Other Titles in the First Past The Post® Series

Verbal Reasoning: Practice Papers (GL)

These books provide real exam practice via four timed tests. These are tailored towards the Granada Learning (GL) Verbal Reasoning assessments but provide invaluable practice for all exam boards. Each test contains a large range of question styles so that, over the four papers, all known questions styles that are likely to come up in the real GL exam are covered. The structure of each test is designed to reflect the likely make-up of the real exam. Full answers and explanations are included.

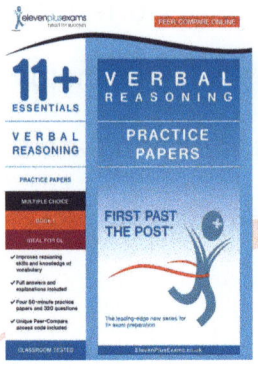

Each test can be marked and evaluated via our Peer-Compare™ Online system, which assesses the candidate's performance anonymously on a question-by-question basis. This helps identify areas for improvement and benchmarks the candidate's score against that of others who have taken the same tests.

Other Titles in the First Past The Post® Series

English: Practice Papers (GL)

These books provide real exam practice via four timed tests. These are tailored towards the Granada Learning (GL) English assessments but provide invaluable practice for all exam boards. Each test comprises a comprehension section and a spelling, punctuation and grammar section, reflecting the likely make-up of the real exam. Full answers and explanations are included.

Each test can be marked and evaluated via our Peer-Compare™ Online system, which assesses the candidate's performance anonymously on a question-by-question basis. This helps identify areas for improvement and benchmarks the candidate's score against that of others who have taken the same tests.

Other Titles in the First Past The Post® Series

Mathematics: Practice Papers (GL)

These books provide real exam practice via four timed tests. These are tailored towards the Granada Learning (GL) Mathematics assessments but provide invaluable practice for all exam boards. Each test covers a large range of topics so that, over the four papers, all known maths topics that are likely to come up in the real GL exam are covered. The structure of each test is designed to reflect the likely make-up of the real exam. Full answers and explanations are included.

Each test can be marked and evaluated via our Peer-Compare™ Online system, which assesses the candidate's performance anonymously on a question-by-question basis. This helps identify areas for improvement and benchmarks the candidate's score against that of others who have taken the same tests.